KYRGYZ
VOCABULARY

ENGLISH-
KYRGYZ

The most useful words
To expand your lexicon and sharpen
your language skills

5000 words

Kyrgyz vocabulary for English speakers - 5000 words
By Andrey Taranov

T&P Books vocabularies are intended for helping you learn, memorize and review foreign words. The dictionary is divided into themes, covering all major spheres of everyday activities, business, science, culture, etc.

The process of learning words using T&P Books' theme-based dictionaries gives you the following advantages:

- Correctly grouped source information predetermines success at subsequent stages of word memorization
- Availability of words derived from the same root allowing memorization of word units (rather than separate words)
- Small units of words facilitate the process of establishing associative links needed for consolidation of vocabulary
- Level of language knowledge can be estimated by the number of learned words

T&P Books Publishing
www.tpbooks.com

ISBN: 978-1-78767-012-9

This book is also available in E-book formats.
Please visit www.tpbooks.com or the major online bookstores.

KYRGYZ VOCABULARY
for English speakers

T&P Books vocabularies are intended to help you learn, memorize, and review foreign words. The vocabulary contains over 5000 commonly used words arranged thematically.

- Vocabulary contains the most commonly used words
- Recommended as an addition to any language course
- Meets the needs of beginners and advanced learners of foreign languages
- Convenient for daily use, revision sessions, and self-testing activities
- Allows you to assess your vocabulary

Special features of the vocabulary

- Words are organized according to their meaning, not alphabetically
- Words are presented in three columns to facilitate the reviewing and self-testing processes
- Words in groups are divided into small blocks to facilitate the learning process
- The vocabulary offers a convenient and simple transcription of each foreign word

The vocabulary has 155 topics including:

Basic Concepts, Numbers, Colors, Months, Seasons, Units of Measurement, Clothing & Accessories, Food & Nutrition, Restaurant, Family Members, Relatives, Character, Feelings, Emotions, Diseases, City, Town, Sightseeing, Shopping, Money, House, Home, Office, Working in the Office, Import & Export, Marketing, Job Search, Sports, Education, Computer, Internet, Tools, Nature, Countries, Nationalities and more ...

T&P BOOKS' THEME-BASED DICTIONARIES

The Correct System for Memorizing Foreign Words

Acquiring vocabulary is one of the most important elements of learning a foreign language, because words allow us to express our thoughts, ask questions, and provide answers. An inadequate vocabulary can impede communication with a foreigner and make it difficult to understand a book or movie well.

The pace of activity in all spheres of modern life, including the learning of modern languages, has increased. Today, we need to memorize large amounts of information (grammar rules, foreign words, etc.) within a short period. However, this does not need to be difficult. All you need to do is to choose the right training materials, learn a few special techniques, and develop your individual training system.

Having a system is critical to the process of language learning. Many people fail to succeed in this regard; they cannot master a foreign language because they fail to follow a system comprised of selecting materials, organizing lessons, arranging new words to be learned, and so on. The lack of a system causes confusion and eventually, lowers self-confidence.

T&P Books' theme-based dictionaries can be included in the list of elements needed for creating an effective system for learning foreign words. These dictionaries were specially developed for learning purposes and are meant to help students effectively memorize words and expand their vocabulary.

Generally speaking, the process of learning words consists of three main elements:

- Reception (creation or acquisition) of a training material, such as a word list
- Work aimed at memorizing new words
- Work aimed at reviewing the learned words, such as self-testing

All three elements are equally important since they determine the quality of work and the final result. All three processes require certain skills and a well-thought-out approach.

New words are often encountered quite randomly when learning a foreign language and it may be difficult to include them all in a unified list. As a result, these words remain written on scraps of paper, in book margins, textbooks, and so on. In order to systematize such words, we have to create and continually update a "book of new words." A paper notebook, a netbook, or a tablet PC can be used for these purposes.

This "book of new words" will be your personal, unique list of words. However, it will only contain the words that you came across during the learning process. For example, you might have written down the words "Sunday," "Tuesday," and "Friday." However, there are additional words for days of the week, for example, "Saturday," that are missing, and your list of words would be incomplete. Using a theme dictionary, in addition to the "book of new words," is a reasonable solution to this problem.

The theme-based dictionary may serve as the basis for expanding your vocabulary.

It will be your big "book of new words" containing the most frequently used words of a foreign language already included. There are quite a few theme-based dictionaries available, and you should ensure that you make the right choice in order to get the maximum benefit from your purchase.

Therefore, we suggest using theme-based dictionaries from T&P Books Publishing as an aid to learning foreign words. Our books are specially developed for effective use in the sphere of vocabulary systematization, expansion and review.

Theme-based dictionaries are not a magical solution to learning new words. However, they can serve as your main database to aid foreign-language acquisition. Apart from theme dictionaries, you can have copybooks for writing down new words, flash cards, glossaries for various texts, as well as other resources; however, a good theme dictionary will always remain your primary collection of words.

T&P Books' theme-based dictionaries are specialty books that contain the most frequently used words in a language.

The main characteristic of such dictionaries is the division of words into themes. For example, the *City* theme contains the words "street," "crossroads," "square," "fountain," and so on. The *Talking* theme might contain words like "to talk," "to ask," "question," and "answer".

All the words in a theme are divided into smaller units, each comprising 3–5 words. Such an arrangement improves the perception of words and makes the learning process less tiresome. Each unit contains a selection of words with similar meanings or identical roots. This allows you to learn words in small groups and establish other associative links that have a positive effect on memorization.

The words on each page are placed in three columns: a word in your native language, its translation, and its transcription. Such positioning allows for the use of techniques for effective memorization. After closing the translation column, you can flip through and review foreign words, and vice versa. "This is an easy and convenient method of review – one that we recommend you do often."

Our theme-based dictionaries contain transcriptions for all the foreign words. Unfortunately, none of the existing transcriptions are able to convey the exact nuances of foreign pronunciation. That is why we recommend using the transcriptions only as a supplementary learning aid. Correct pronunciation can only be acquired with the help of sound. Therefore our collection includes audio theme-based dictionaries.

The process of learning words using T&P Books' theme-based dictionaries gives you the following advantages:

- You have correctly grouped source information, which predetermines your success at subsequent stages of word memorization
- Availability of words derived from the same root (lazy, lazily, lazybones), allowing you to memorize word units instead of separate words
- Small units of words facilitate the process of establishing associative links needed for consolidation of vocabulary
- You can estimate the number of learned words and hence your level of language knowledge
- The dictionary allows for the creation of an effective and high-quality revision process
- You can revise certain themes several times, modifying the revision methods and techniques
- Audio versions of the dictionaries help you to work out the pronunciation of words and develop your skills of auditory word perception

The T&P Books' theme-based dictionaries are offered in several variants differing in the number of words: 1.500, 3.000, 5.000, 7.000, and 9.000 words. There are also dictionaries containing 15,000 words for some language combinations. Your choice of dictionary will depend on your knowledge level and goals.

We sincerely believe that our dictionaries will become your trusty assistant in learning foreign languages and will allow you to easily acquire the necessary vocabulary.

TABLE OF CONTENTS

T&P Books' Theme-Based Dictionaries 4
Pronunciation guide 13
Abbreviations 14

BASIC CONCEPTS 15
Basic concepts. Part 1 15

1. Pronouns 15
2. Greetings. Salutations. Farewells 15
3. How to address 16
4. Cardinal numbers. Part 1 16
5. Cardinal numbers. Part 2 17
6. Ordinal numbers 18
7. Numbers. Fractions 18
8. Numbers. Basic operations 18
9. Numbers. Miscellaneous 19
10. The most important verbs. Part 1 19
11. The most important verbs. Part 2 20
12. The most important verbs. Part 3 21
13. The most important verbs. Part 4 22
14. Colors 23
15. Questions 24
16. Prepositions 25
17. Function words. Adverbs. Part 1 25
18. Function words. Adverbs. Part 2 27

Basic concepts. Part 2 29

19. Weekdays 29
20. Hours. Day and night 29
21. Months. Seasons 30
22. Units of measurement 32
23. Containers 33

HUMAN BEING 35
Human being. The body 35

24. Head 35
25. Human body 36

Clothing & Accessories   38

26. Outerwear. Coats   38
27. Men's & women's clothing   38
28. Clothing. Underwear   39
29. Headwear   39
30. Footwear   40
31. Personal accessories   40
32. Clothing. Miscellaneous   41
33. Personal care. Cosmetics   41
34. Watches. Clocks   42

Food. Nutricion   44

35. Food   44
36. Drinks   46
37. Vegetables   47
38. Fruits. Nuts   47
39. Bread. Candy   48
40. Cooked dishes   49
41. Spices   50
42. Meals   50
43. Table setting   51
44. Restaurant   52

Family, relatives and friends   53

45. Personal information. Forms   53
46. Family members. Relatives   53

Medicine   55

47. Diseases   55
48. Symptoms. Treatments. Part 1   56
49. Symptoms. Treatments. Part 2   57
50. Symptoms. Treatments. Part 3   58
51. Doctors   59
52. Medicine. Drugs. Accessories   59

HUMAN HABITAT   61
City   61

53. City. Life in the city   61
54. Urban institutions   62
55. Signs   64
56. Urban transportation   65

57.	Sightseeing	66
58.	Shopping	66
59.	Money	67
60.	Post. Postal service	68

Dwelling. House. Home   70

61.	House. Electricity	70
62.	Villa. Mansion	70
63.	Apartment	71
64.	Furniture. Interior	71
65.	Bedding	72
66.	Kitchen	72
67.	Bathroom	73
68.	Household appliances	74

HUMAN ACTIVITIES   76
Job. Business. Part 1   76

69.	Office. Working in the office	76
70.	Business processes. Part 1	77
71.	Business processes. Part 2	78
72.	Production. Works	79
73.	Contract. Agreement	81
74.	Import & Export	81
75.	Finances	82
76.	Marketing	83
77.	Advertising	83
78.	Banking	84
79.	Telephone. Phone conversation	85
80.	Cell phone	85
81.	Stationery	86
82.	Kinds of business	86

Job. Business. Part 2   89

83.	Show. Exhibition	89
84.	Science. Research. Scientists	90

Professions and occupations   92

85.	Job search. Dismissal	92
86.	Business people	92
87.	Service professions	94
88.	Military professions and ranks	95
89.	Officials. Priests	95

90. Agricultural professions   96
91. Art professions   96
92. Various professions   97
93. Occupations. Social status   98

Education   100

94. School   100
95. College. University   101
96. Sciences. Disciplines   102
97. Writing system. Orthography   102
98. Foreign languages   104

Rest. Entertainment. Travel   106

99. Trip. Travel   106
100. Hotel   107

TECHNICAL EQUIPMENT. TRANSPORTATION   108
Technical equipment   108

101. Computer   108
102. Internet. E-mail   109
103. Electricity   110
104. Tools   111

Transportation   114

105. Airplane   114
106. Train   115
107. Ship   116
108. Airport   118

Life events   119

109. Holidays. Event   119
110. Funerals. Burial   120
111. War. Soldiers   121
112. War. Military actions. Part 1   122
113. War. Military actions. Part 2   123
114. Weapons   125
115. Ancient people   126
116. Middle Ages   127
117. Leader. Chief. Authorities   129
118. Breaking the law. Criminals. Part 1   129
119. Breaking the law. Criminals. Part 2   131

120. Police. Law. Part 1   132
121. Police. Law. Part 2   133

NATURE   135
The Earth. Part 1   135

122. Outer space   135
123. The Earth   136
124. Cardinal directions   137
125. Sea. Ocean   137
126. Seas' and Oceans' names   138
127. Mountains   139
128. Mountains names   140
129. Rivers   140
130. Rivers' names   141
131. Forest   142
132. Natural resources   143

The Earth. Part 2   145

133. Weather   145
134. Severe weather. Natural disasters   146

Fauna   147

135. Mammals. Predators   147
136. Wild animals   147
137. Domestic animals   149
138. Birds   150
139. Fish. Marine animals   151
140. Amphibians. Reptiles   152
141. Insects   152

Flora   154

142. Trees   154
143. Shrubs   155
144. Fruits. Berries   155
145. Flowers. Plants   156
146. Cereals, grains   157

COUNTRIES. NATIONALITIES   158

147. Western Europe   158
148. Central and Eastern Europe   158
149. Former USSR countries   159

150.	Asia	159
151.	North America	160
152.	Central and South America	160
153.	Africa	161
154.	Australia. Oceania	161
155.	Cities	161

PRONUNCIATION GUIDE

T&P phonetic alphabet	Kyrgyz example	English example
[a]	манжа [mandʒa]	shorter than in ask
[e]	келечек [keletʃek]	elm, medal
[i]	жигит [dʒigit]	shorter than in feet
[ɪ]	кубаныч [kubanɪtʃ]	big, America
[o]	мактоо [maktoo]	pod, John
[u]	узундук [uzunduk]	book
[ʉ]	алюминий [alʉminij]	youth, usually
[y]	түнкү [tynky]	fuel, tuna
[b]	ашкабак [aʃkabak]	baby, book
[d]	адам [adam]	day, doctor
[dʒ]	жыгач [dʒɪgatʃ]	joke, general
[f]	флейта [flejta]	face, food
[g]	тегерек [tegerek]	game, gold
[j]	бөйрөк [bøjrøk]	yes, New York
[k]	карапа [karapa]	clock, kiss
[l]	алтын [altɪn]	lace, people
[m]	бешмант [beʃmant]	magic, milk
[n]	найза [najza]	name, normal
[ŋ]	булуң [buluŋ]	ring
[p]	пайдубал [pajdubal]	pencil, private
[r]	рахмат [raχmat]	rice, radio
[s]	сагызган [sagɪzgan]	city, boss
[ʃ]	бурулуш [buruluʃ]	machine, shark
[t]	түтүн [tytyn]	tourist, trip
[χ]	пахтадан [paχtadan]	hot, hobby
[ts]	шприц [ʃprits]	cats, tsetse fly
[tʃ]	биринчи [birintʃi]	church, French
[v]	квартал [kvartal]	very, river
[z]	казуу [kazuu]	zebra, please
[ʲ]	руль, актёр [rulʲ, aktʲor]	palatalization sign

13

ABBREVIATIONS
used in the vocabulary

English abbreviations

ab.	-	about
adj	-	adjective
adv	-	adverb
anim.	-	animate
as adj	-	attributive noun used as adjective
e.g.	-	for example
etc.	-	et cetera
fam.	-	familiar
fem.	-	feminine
form.	-	formal
inanim.	-	inanimate
masc.	-	masculine
math	-	mathematics
mil.	-	military
n	-	noun
pl	-	plural
pron.	-	pronoun
sb	-	somebody
sing.	-	singular
sth	-	something
v aux	-	auxiliary verb
vi	-	intransitive verb
vi, vt	-	intransitive, transitive verb
vt	-	transitive verb

BASIC CONCEPTS

Basic concepts. Part 1

1. Pronouns

I, me	мен, мага	men, maga
you	сен	sen
he, she, it	ал	al
we	биз	biz
you (to a group)	силер	siler
you (polite, sing.)	сиз	siz
you (polite, pl)	сиздер	sizder
they	алар	alar

2. Greetings. Salutations. Farewells

Hello! (fam.)	Салам!	salam!
Hello! (form.)	Саламатсызбы!	salamatsızbı!
Good morning!	Кутман таңыңыз менен!	kutman taŋıŋız menen!
Good afternoon!	Кутман күнүңүз менен!	kutman kynyŋyz menen!
Good evening!	Кутман кечиңиз менен!	kutman ketʃiŋiz menen!
to say hello	учурашуу	utʃuraʃuu
Hi! (hello)	Кандай!	kandaj!
greeting (n)	салам	salam
to greet (vt)	саламдашуу	salamdaʃuu
How are you?	Иштериң кандай?	iʃteriŋ kandaj?
How are you? (form.)	Иштериңиз кандай?	iʃteriŋiz kandaj?
How are you? (fam.)	Иштер кандай?	iʃter kandaj?
What's new?	Эмне жаңылык?	emne dʒaŋılık?
Bye-Bye! Goodbye!	Көрүшкөнчө!	køryʃkøntʃø!
See you soon!	Эмки жолукканга чейин!	emki dʒolukkanga tʃejin!
Farewell! (to a friend)	Кош бол!	koʃ bol!
Farewell! (form.)	кырк бир	kırk bir
to say goodbye	коштошуу	koʃtoʃuu
So long!	Жакшы кал!	dʒakʃı kal!
Thank you!	Рахмат!	raχmat!
Thank you very much!	Чоң рахмат!	tʃoŋ raχmat!
You're welcome	Эч нерсе эмес	etʃ nerse emes

| Don't mention it! | Алкышка арзыбайт | alkıʃka arzıbajt |
| It was nothing | Эчтеке эмес. | etʃteke emes |

Excuse me! (fam.)	Кечир!	ketʃir!
Excuse me! (form.)	Кечирип коюңузчу!	ketʃirip kojuŋuztʃu!
to excuse (forgive)	кечирүү	ketʃiryy
to apologize (vi)	кечирим суроо	ketʃirim suroo
My apologies	Кечирим сурайм.	ketʃirim surajm
I'm sorry!	Кечиресиз!	ketʃiresiz!
to forgive (vt)	кечирүү	ketʃiryy
It's okay! (that's all right)	Эч капачылык жок.	etʃ kapatʃılık dʒok
please (adv)	суранам	suranam

Don't forget!	Унутуп калбаңыз!	unutup kalbaŋız!
Certainly!	Албетте!	albette!
Of course not!	Албетте жок!	albette dʒok!
Okay! (I agree)	Макул!	makul!
That's enough!	Жетишет!	dʒetiʃet!

3. How to address

Excuse me, ...	Кечиресиз!	ketʃiresiz!
mister, sir	мырза	mırza
ma'am	айым	ajım
miss	чоң кыз	tʃoŋ kız
young man	чоң жигит	tʃoŋ dʒigit
young man (little boy, kid)	жаш бала	dʒaʃ bala
miss (little girl)	кызым	kızım

4. Cardinal numbers. Part 1

0 zero	нөл	nøl
1 one	бир	bir
2 two	эки	eki
3 three	үч	ytʃ
4 four	төрт	tørt

5 five	беш	beʃ
6 six	алты	altı
7 seven	жети	dʒeti
8 eight	сегиз	segiz
9 nine	тогуз	toguz

10 ten	он	on
11 eleven	он бир	on bir
12 twelve	он эки	on eki
13 thirteen	он үч	on ytʃ
14 fourteen	он төрт	on tørt

15 fifteen	он беш	on beʃ
16 sixteen	он алты	on altı
17 seventeen	он жети	on dʒeti
18 eighteen	он сегиз	on segiz
19 nineteen	он тогуз	on toguz
20 twenty	жыйырма	dʒıjırma
21 twenty-one	жыйырма бир	dʒıjırma bir
22 twenty-two	жыйырма эки	dʒıjırma eki
23 twenty-three	жыйырма үч	dʒıjırma ytʃ
30 thirty	отуз	otuz
31 thirty-one	отуз бир	otuz bir
32 thirty-two	отуз эки	otuz eki
33 thirty-three	отуз үч	otuz ytʃ
40 forty	кырк	kırk
42 forty-two	кырк эки	kırk eki
43 forty-three	кырк үч	kırk ytʃ
50 fifty	элүү	elyy
51 fifty-one	элүү бир	elyy bir
52 fifty-two	элүү эки	elyy eki
53 fifty-three	элүү үч	elyy ytʃ
60 sixty	алтымыш	altımıʃ
61 sixty-one	алтымыш бир	altımıʃ bir
62 sixty-two	алтымыш эки	altımıʃ eki
63 sixty-three	алтымыш үч	altımıʃ ytʃ
70 seventy	жетимиш	dʒetimiʃ
71 seventy-one	жетимиш бир	dʒetimiʃ bir
72 seventy-two	жетимиш эки	dʒetimiʃ eki
73 seventy-three	жетимиш үч	dʒetimiʃ ytʃ
80 eighty	сексен	seksen
81 eighty-one	сексен бир	seksen bir
82 eighty-two	сексен эки	seksen eki
83 eighty-three	сексен үч	seksen ytʃ
90 ninety	токсон	tokson
91 ninety-one	токсон бир	tokson bir
92 ninety-two	токсон эки	tokson eki
93 ninety-three	токсон үч	tokson ytʃ

5. Cardinal numbers. Part 2

100 one hundred	бир жүз	bir dʒyz
200 two hundred	эки жүз	eki dʒyz
300 three hundred	үч жүз	ytʃ dʒyz

400 four hundred	төрт жүз	tørt dʒyz
500 five hundred	беш жүз	beʃ dʒyz
600 six hundred	алты жүз	altı dʒyz
700 seven hundred	жети жүз	dʒeti dʒyz
800 eight hundred	сегиз жүз	segiz dʒyz
900 nine hundred	тогуз жүз	toguz dʒyz
1000 one thousand	бир миң	bir miŋ
2000 two thousand	эки миң	eki miŋ
3000 three thousand	үч миң	ytʃ miŋ
10000 ten thousand	он миң	on miŋ
one hundred thousand	жүз миң	dʒyz miŋ
million	миллион	million
billion	миллиард	milliard

6. Ordinal numbers

first (adj)	биринчи	birintʃi
second (adj)	экинчи	ekintʃi
third (adj)	үчүнчү	ytʃyntʃy
fourth (adj)	төртүнчү	tørtyntʃy
fifth (adj)	бешинчи	beʃintʃi
sixth (adj)	алтынчы	altıntʃı
seventh (adj)	жетинчи	dʒetintʃi
eighth (adj)	сегизинчи	segizintʃi
ninth (adj)	тогузунчу	toguzuntʃu
tenth (adj)	онунчу	onuntʃu

7. Numbers. Fractions

fraction	бөлчөк	bøltʃøk
one half	экиден бир	ekiden bir
one third	үчтөн бир	ytʃtøn bir
one quarter	төрттөн бир	tørttøn bir
one eighth	сегизден бир	segizden bir
one tenth	тогуздан бир	toguzdan bir
two thirds	үчтөн эки	ytʃtøn eki
three quarters	төрттөн үч	tørttøn ytʃ

8. Numbers. Basic operations

subtraction	кемитүү	kemityy
to subtract (vi, vt)	кемитүү	kemityy

division	бөлүү	bølyy
to divide (vt)	бөлүү	bølyy

addition	кошуу	koʃuu
to add up (vt)	кошуу	koʃuu
to add (vi, vt)	кошуу	koʃuu
multiplication	көбөйтүү	købøjtyy
to multiply (vt)	көбөйтүү	købøjtyy

9. Numbers. Miscellaneous

digit, figure	санарип	sanarip
number	сан	san
numeral	сан атооч	san atootʃ
minus sign	кемитүү	kemityy
plus sign	плюс	plʉs
formula	формула	formula

calculation	эсептөө	eseptøø
to count (vi, vt)	саноо	sanoo
to count up	эсептөө	eseptøø
to compare (vt)	салыштыруу	salıʃtıruu

How much?	Канча?	kantʃa?
sum, total	жыйынтык	dʒıjıntık
result	натыйжа	natıjdʒa
remainder	калдык	kaldık

a few (e.g., ~ years ago)	бир нече	bir netʃe
little (I had ~ time)	биртике	bir az
few (I have ~ friends)	бир аз	bir az
a little (~ water)	кичине	kitʃine
the rest	калганы	kalganı
one and a half	бир жарым	bir dʒarım
dozen	он эки даана	on eki daana

in half (adv)	тең экиге	teŋ ekige
equally (evenly)	тең	teŋ
half	жарым	dʒarım
time (three ~s)	бир жолу	bir dʒolu

10. The most important verbs. Part 1

to advise (vt)	кеңеш берүү	keŋeʃ beryy
to agree (say yes)	макул болуу	makul boluu
to answer (vi, vt)	жооп берүү	dʒoop beryy
to apologize (vi)	кечирим суроо	ketʃirim suroo
to arrive (vi)	келүү	kelyy

to ask (~ oneself)	суроо	suroo
to ask (~ sb to do sth)	суроо	suroo
to be (vi)	болуу	boluu

to be afraid	жазкануу	dʒazkanuu
to be hungry	ачка болуу	atʃka boluu
to be interested in …	… кызыгуу	… kızıguu
to be needed	керек болуу	kerek boluu
to be surprised	таң калуу	taŋ kaluu

to be thirsty	суусап калуу	suusap kaluu
to begin (vt)	баштоо	baʃtoo
to belong to …	таандык болуу	taandık boluu
to boast (vi)	мактануу	maktanuu
to break (split into pieces)	сындыруу	sındıruu

to call (~ for help)	чакыруу	tʃakıruu
can (v aux)	жасай алуу	dʒasaj aluu
to catch (vt)	кармоо	karmoo
to change (vt)	өзгөртүү	øzgørtyy
to choose (select)	тандоо	tandoo

to come down (the stairs)	ылдый түшүү	ıldıj tyʃyy
to compare (vt)	салыштыруу	salıʃtıruu
to complain (vi, vt)	арызлануу	arızdanuu
to confuse (mix up)	адаштыруу	adaʃtıruu
to continue (vt)	улантуу	ulantuu
to control (vt)	башкаруу	baʃkaruu

to cook (dinner)	тамак бышыруу	tamak bıʃıruu
to cost (vt)	туруу	turuu
to count (add up)	саноо	sanoo
to count on …	… ишенүү	… iʃenyy
to create (vt)	жаратуу	dʒaratuu
to cry (weep)	ыйлоо	ıjloo

11. The most important verbs. Part 2

to deceive (vi, vt)	алдоо	aldoo
to decorate (tree, street)	кооздоо	koozdoo
to defend (a country, etc.)	коргоо	korgoo
to demand (request firmly)	талап кылуу	talap kıluu
to dig (vt)	казуу	kazuu

to discuss (vt)	талкуулоо	talkuuloo
to do (vt)	кылуу	kıluu
to doubt (have doubts)	күмөн саноо	kymøn sanoo
to drop (let fall)	түшүрүп алуу	tyʃyryp aluu
to enter (room, house, etc.)	кирүү	kiryy

to excuse (forgive)	кечирүү	ketʃiryy
to exist (vi)	чыгуу	tʃiguu
to expect (foresee)	күтүү	kytyy
to explain (vt)	түшүндүрүү	tyʃyndyryy
to fall (vi)	жыгылуу	dʒıgıluu

to find (vt)	таап алуу	taap aluu
to finish (vt)	бүтүрүү	bytyryy
to fly (vi)	учуу	utʃuu
to follow ... (come after)	... ээрчүү	... eertʃyy
to forget (vi, vt)	унутуу	unutuu

to forgive (vt)	кечирүү	ketʃiryy
to give (vt)	берүү	beryy
to give a hint	четин чыгаруу	tʃetin tʃigaruu
to go (on foot)	жөө басуу	dʒөө basuu

to go for a swim	сууга түшүү	suuga tyʃyy
to go out (for dinner, etc.)	чыгуу	tʃiguu
to guess (the answer)	жандырмагын табуу	dʒandırmagın tabuu

to have (vt)	бар болуу	bar boluu
to have breakfast	эртең менен тамактануу	erteŋ menen tamaktanuu
to have dinner	кечки тамакты ичүү	ketʃki tamaktı itʃyy
to have lunch	түштөнүү	tyʃtөnyy
to hear (vt)	угуу	uguu

to help (vt)	жардам берүү	dʒardam beryy
to hide (vt)	жашыруу	dʒaʃiruu
to hope (vi, vt)	үмүттөнүү	ymyttөnyy
to hunt (vi, vt)	аңчылык кылуу	aŋtʃilik kıluu
to hurry (vi)	шашуу	ʃaʃuu

12. The most important verbs. Part 3

to inform (vt)	маалымат берүү	maalımat beryy
to insist (vi, vt)	көшөрүү	köʃөryy
to insult (vt)	кемсинтүү	kemsintyy
to invite (vt)	чакыруу	tʃakıruu
to joke (vi)	тамашалоо	tamaʃaloo

to keep (vt)	сактоо	saktoo
to keep silent, to hush	үнчүкпоо	untʃukpoo
to kill (vt)	өлтүрүү	öltyryy
to know (sb)	таануу	taanuu
to know (sth)	билүү	bilyy
to laugh (vi)	күлүү	kylyy
to liberate (city, etc.)	бошотуу	boʃotuu
to like (I like ...)	жактыруу	dʒaktıruu

to look for ... (search)	... издөө	... izdøø
to love (sb)	сүйүү	syjyy
to make a mistake	ката кетирүү	kata ketiryy

to manage, to run	башкаруу	baʃkaruu
to mean (signify)	билдирүү	bildiryy
to mention (talk about)	айтып өтүү	ajtıp øtyy
to miss (school, etc.)	калтыруу	kaltıruu
to notice (see)	байкоо	bajkoo

to object (vi, vt)	каршы болуу	karʃı boluu
to observe (see)	байкоо салуу	bajkoo
to open (vt)	ачуу	atʃuu
to order (meal, etc.)	буйрутма кылуу	bujrutma kıluu
to order (mil.)	буйрук кылуу	bujruk kıluu
to own (possess)	ээ болуу	ee boluu

to participate (vi)	катышуу	katıʃuu
to pay (vi, vt)	төлөө	tøløø
to permit (vt)	уруксат берүү	uruksat beryy
to plan (vt)	пландаштыруу	plandaʃtıruu
to play (children)	ойноо	ojnoo

to pray (vi, vt)	дуба кылуу	duba kıluu
to prefer (vt)	артык көрүү	artık køryy
to promise (vt)	убада берүү	ubada beryy
to pronounce (vt)	айтуу	ajtuu
to propose (vt)	сунуштоо	sunuʃtoo
to punish (vt)	жазалоо	dʒazaloo

13. The most important verbs. Part 4

to read (vi, vt)	окуу	okuu
to recommend (vt)	сунуштоо	sunuʃtoo
to refuse (vi, vt)	баш тартуу	baʃ tartuu
to regret (be sorry)	өкүнүү	økynyy
to rent (sth from sb)	батирге алуу	batirge aluu

to repeat (say again)	кайталоо	kajtaloo
to reserve, to book	камдык буйрутмалоо	kamdık bujrutmaloo
to run (vi)	чуркоо	tʃurkoo
to save (rescue)	куткаруу	kutkaruu
to say (~ thank you)	айтуу	ajtuu

to scold (vt)	урушуу	uruʃuu
to see (vt)	көрүү	køryy
to sell (vt)	сатуу	satuu
to send (vt)	жөнөтүү	dʒønøtyy
to shoot (vi)	атуу	atuu
to shout (vi)	кыйкыруу	kıjkıruu

to show (vt)	көрсөтүү	kørsøtyy
to sign (document)	кол коюу	kol kojʉu
to sit down (vi)	отуруу	oturuu

to smile (vi)	жылмаюу	dʒɪlmadʒʉu
to speak (vi, vt)	сүйлөө	syjløø
to steal (money, etc.)	уурдоо	uurdoo
to stop (for pause, etc.)	токтоо	toktoo
to stop (please ~ calling me)	токтотуу	toktotuu

to study (vt)	окуу	okuu
to swim (vi)	сүзүү	syzyy
to take (vt)	алуу	aluu
to think (vi, vt)	ойлоо	ojloo
to threaten (vt)	коркутуу	korkutuu

to touch (with hands)	тийүү	tijyy
to translate (vt)	которуу	kotoruu
to trust (vt)	ишенүү	iʃenyy
to try (attempt)	аракет кылуу	araket kɪluu
to turn (e.g., ~ left)	бурулуу	buruluu

to underestimate (vt)	баалабоо	baalaboo
to understand (vt)	түшүнүү	tyʃynyy
to unite (vt)	бириктирүү	biriktiryy
to wait (vt)	күтүү	kytyy

to want (wish, desire)	каалоо	kaaloo
to warn (vt)	эскертүү	eskertyy
to work (vi)	иштөө	iʃtøø
to write (vt)	жазуу	dʒazuu
to write down	кагазга түшүрүү	kagazga tyʃyryy

14. Colors

color	түс	tys
shade (tint)	кошумча түс	koʃumtʃa tys
hue	кубулуу	kubuluu
rainbow	күндүн кулагы	kyndyn kulagɪ

white (adj)	ак	ak
black (adj)	кара	kara
gray (adj)	боз	boz

green (adj)	жашыл	dʒaʃɪl
yellow (adj)	сары	sarɪ
red (adj)	кызыл	kɪzɪl
blue (adj)	көк	køk
light blue (adj)	көгүлтүр	køgyltyr

pink (adj)	мала	mala
orange (adj)	кызгылт сары	kızgılt sarı
violet (adj)	сыя көк	sıja køk
brown (adj)	күрөң	kyrøŋ

| golden (adj) | алтын түстүү | altın tystyy |
| silvery (adj) | күмүш өңдүү | kymyʃ øŋdyy |

beige (adj)	сары боз	sarı boz
cream (adj)	саргылт	sargılt
turquoise (adj)	бирюза	birɥza
cherry red (adj)	кочкул кызыл	kotʃkul kızıl
lilac (adj)	кызгылт көгүш	kızgılt køgyʃ
crimson (adj)	ачык кызыл	atʃık kızıl

light (adj)	ачык	atʃık
dark (adj)	күңүрт	kyŋyrt
bright, vivid (adj)	ачык	atʃık

colored (pencils)	түстүү	tystyy
color (e.g., ~ film)	түстүү	tystyy
black-and-white (adj)	ак-кара	ak-kara
plain (one-colored)	бир өңчөй түстө	bir øŋtʃøj tystø
multicolored (adj)	ар түрдүү түстө	ar tyrdyy tystø

15. Questions

Who?	Ким?	kim?
What?	Эмне?	emne?
Where? (at, in)	Каерде?	kaerde?
Where (to)?	Каяка?	kajaka?
From where?	Каяктан?	kajaktan?
When?	Качан?	katʃan?
Why? (What for?)	Эмне үчүн?	emne ytʃyn?
Why? (~ are you crying?)	Эмнеге?	emnege?

What for?	Кайсы керекке?	kajsı kerekke?
How? (in what way)	Кандай?	kandaj?
What? (What kind of ...?)	Кайсы?	kajsı?
Which?	Кайсынысы?	kajsınısı?

To whom?	Кимге?	kimge?
About whom?	Ким жөнүндө?	kim dʒønyndø?
About what?	Эмне жөнүндө?	emne dʒønyndø?
With whom?	Ким менен?	kim menen?

How many? How much?	Канча?	kantʃa?
Whose?	Кимдики?	kimdiki?
Whose? (fem.)	Кимдики?	kimdiki?
Whose? (pl)	Кимдердики?	kimderdiki?

16. Prepositions

with (accompanied by)	менен	menen
without	-сыз, -сиз	-sız, -siz
to (indicating direction)	,,, кездей	… køzdøj
about (talking ~ …)	… жөнүндө	… dʒønyndø
before (in time)	… астында	… astında
in front of …	… алдында	… aldında
under (beneath, below)	… астында	… astında
above (over)	… ейде	… øjdø
on (atop)	… үстүндө	… ystyndø
from (off, out of)	-дан	-dan
of (made from)	-дан	-dan
in (e.g., ~ ten minutes)	… ичинде	… itʃinde
over (across the top of)	… үстүнөн	… ystynøn

17. Function words. Adverbs. Part 1

Where? (at, in)	Каерде?	kaerde?
here (adv)	бул жерде	bul dʒerde
there (adv)	тээтигил жакта	teetigil dʒakta
somewhere (to be)	бир жерде	bir dʒerde
nowhere (not in any place)	эч жакта	etʃ dʒakta
by (near, beside)	… жанында	… dʒanında
by the window	терезенин жанында	terezenin dʒanında
Where (to)?	Каяка?	kajaka?
here (e.g., come ~!)	бери	beri
there (e.g., to go ~)	нары	narı
from here (adv)	бул жерден	bul dʒerden
from there (adv)	тигил жерден	tigil dʒerden
close (adv)	жакын	dʒakın
far (adv)	алыс	alıs
near (e.g., ~ Paris)	… тегерегинде	… tegereginde
nearby (adv)	жакын арада	dʒakın arada
not far (adv)	алыс эмес	alıs emes
left (adj)	сол	sol
on the left	сол жакта	sol dʒakta
to the left	солго	solgo
right (adj)	оң	oŋ
on the right	оң жакта	oŋ dʒakta

to the right	оңго	ongo
in front (adv)	астыда	astıda
front (as adj)	алдыңкы	aldıŋkı
ahead (the kids ran ~)	алдыга	aldıga

behind (adv)	артында	artında
from behind	артынан	artınan
back (towards the rear)	артка	artka

| middle | ортосу | ortosu |
| in the middle | ортосунда | ortosunda |

at the side	капталында	kaptalında
everywhere (adv)	бүт жерде	byt dʒerde
around (in all directions)	айланасында	ajlanasında

from inside	ичинде	itʃinde
somewhere (to go)	бир жерде	bir dʒerde
straight (directly)	түз	tyz
back (e.g., come ~)	кайра	kajra

| from anywhere | бир жерден | bir dʒerden |
| from somewhere | бир жактан | bir dʒaktan |

firstly (adv)	биринчиден	birintʃiden
secondly (adv)	экинчиден	ekintʃiden
thirdly (adv)	үчүнчүдөн	ytʃyntʃydøn

suddenly (adv)	күтпөгөн жерден	kytpøgøn dʒerden
at first (in the beginning)	башында	baʃında
for the first time	биринчи жолу	birintʃi dʒolu
long before ...	... алдында	... aldında
anew (over again)	башынан	baʃınan
for good (adv)	түбөлүккө	tybølykkø

never (adv)	эч качан	etʃ katʃan
again (adv)	кайра	kajra
now (at present)	эми	emi
often (adv)	көпчүлүк учурда	køptʃylyk utʃurda
then (adv)	анда	anda
urgently (quickly)	тезинен	tezinen
usually (adv)	көбүнчө	købyntʃø

by the way, ...	баса, ...	basa, ...
possibly	мүмкүн	mymkyn
probably (adv)	балким	balkim
maybe (adv)	ыктымал	ıktımal
besides ...	андан тышкары, ...	andan tıʃkarı, ...
that's why ...	ошондуктан ...	oʃonduktan ...
in spite of ...	... карабастан	... karabastan
thanks to ...	... күчү менен	... kytʃy menen
what (pron.)	эмне	emne

that (conj.)	эмне	emne
something	бир нерсе	bir nerse
anything (something)	бир нерсе	bir nerse
nothing	эч нерсе	etʃ nerse

who (pron.)	ким	kim
someone	кимдир бироо	kimdir birøø
somebody	бироо жарым	birøø dʒarım

nobody	эч ким	etʃ kim
nowhere (a voyage to ~)	эч жака	etʃ dʒaka
nobody's	эч кимдики	etʃ kimdiki
somebody's	бироонүкү	birøønyky

so (I'm ~ glad)	эми	emi
also (as well)	ошондой эле	oʃondoj ele
too (as well)	дагы	dagı

18. Function words. Adverbs. Part 2

Why?	Эмнеге?	emnege?
for some reason	эмнегедир	emnegedir
because ...	... себептен	... sebepten
for some purpose	эмне үчүндүр	emne ytʃyndyr

and	жана	dʒana
or	же	dʒe
but	бирок	birok
for (e.g., ~ me)	үчүн	ytʃyn

too (~ many people)	өтө эле	øtø ele
only (exclusively)	азыр эле	azır ele
exactly (adv)	так	tak
about (more or less)	болжол менен	boldʒol menen

approximately (adv)	болжол менен	boldʒol menen
approximate (adj)	болжолдуу	boldʒolduu
almost (adv)	дээрлик	deerlik
the rest	калганы	kalganı

the other (second)	башка	baʃka
other (different)	башка болөк	baʃka bøløk
each (adj)	ар бири	ar biri
any (no matter which)	баардык	baardık
many, much (a lot of)	көп	køp
many people	көбү	køby
all (everyone)	баары	baarı

| in return for ... | ... алмашуу | ... almaʃuu |
| in exchange (adv) | ордуна | orduna |

| by hand (made) | колго | kolgo |
| hardly (negative opinion) | ишенүүгө болбойт | iʃenyygø bolbojt |

probably (adv)	балким	balkim
on purpose (intentionally)	атайын	atajın
by accident (adv)	кокустан	kokustan

very (adv)	аябай	ajabaj
for example (adv)	мисалы	misalı
between	ортосунда	ortosunda
among	арасында	arasında
so much (such a lot)	ошончо	oʃontʃo
especially (adv)	өзгөчө	øzgøtʃø

Basic concepts. Part 2

19. Weekdays

Monday	дүйшөмбү	dyjʃømby
Tuesday	шейшемби	ʃejʃembi
Wednesday	шаршемби	ʃarʃembi
Thursday	бейшемби	bejʃembi
Friday	жума	dʒuma
Saturday	ишенби	iʃenbi
Sunday	жекшемби	dʒekʃembi
today (adv)	бүгүн	bygyn
tomorrow (adv)	эртең	erteŋ
the day after tomorrow	бирсүгүнү	birsygyny
yesterday (adv)	кечээ	ketʃee
the day before yesterday	мурда күнү	murda kyny
day	күн	kyn
working day	иш күнү	iʃ kyny
public holiday	майрам күнү	majram kyny
day off	дем алыш күн	dem alıʃ kyn
weekend	дем алыш күндөр	dem alıʃ kyndør
all day long	күнү бою	kyny bojʉ
the next day (adv)	кийинки күнү	kijinki kyny
two days ago	эки күн мурун	eki kyn murun
the day before	жакында	dʒakında
daily (adj)	күндө	kyndø
every day (adv)	күн сайын	kyn sajın
week	жума	dʒuma
last week (adv)	өткөн жумада	øtkøn dʒumada
next week (adv)	келаткан жумада	kelatkan dʒumada
weekly (adj)	жума сайын	dʒuma sajın
every week (adv)	жума сайын	dʒuma sajın
twice a week	жумасына эки жолу	dʒumasına eki dʒolu
every Tuesday	ар шейшемби	ar ʃejʃembi

20. Hours. Day and night

morning	таң	taŋ
in the morning	эртең менен	erteŋ menen
noon, midday	жарым күн	dʒarım kyn

in the afternoon	түштөн кийин	tyʃtøn kijin
evening	кеч	ketʃ
in the evening	кечинде	ketʃinde
night	түн	tyn
at night	түндө	tyndø
midnight	жарым түн	dʒarım tyn
second	секунда	sekunda
minute	мүнөт	mynøt
hour	саат	saat
half an hour	жарым саат	dʒarım saat
a quarter-hour	чейрек саат	tʃejrek saat
fifteen minutes	он беш мүнөт	on beʃ mynøt
24 hours	сутка	sutka
sunrise	күндүн чыгышы	kyndyn tʃıgıʃı
dawn	таң агаруу	taŋ agaruu
early morning	таң эрте	taŋ erte
sunset	күн батуу	kyn batuu
early in the morning	таң эрте	taŋ erte
this morning	бүгүн эртең менен	bygyn erteŋ menen
tomorrow morning	эртең эртең менен	erteŋ erteŋ menen
this afternoon	күндүзү	kyndyzy
in the afternoon	түштөн кийин	tyʃtøn kijin
tomorrow afternoon	эртең түштөн кийин	erteŋ tyʃtøn kijin
tonight (this evening)	бүгүн кечинде	bygyn ketʃinde
tomorrow night	эртең кечинде	erteŋ ketʃinde
at 3 o'clock sharp	туура саат үчтө	tuura saat ytʃtø
about 4 o'clock	болжол менен төрт саат	boldʒol menen tørt saat
by 12 o'clock	саат он экиде	saat on ekide
in 20 minutes	жыйырма мүнөттөн кийин	dʒıjırma mynøttøn kijin
in an hour	бир сааттан кийин	bir saattan kijin
on time (adv)	өз убагында	øz ubagında
a quarter to ...	... он беш мүнөт калды	... on beʃ mynøt kaldı
within an hour	бир сааттын ичинде	bir saattın itʃinde
every 15 minutes	он беш мүнөт сайын	on beʃ mynøt sajın
round the clock	бир сутка бою	bir sutka boju

21. Months. Seasons

January	январь	janvarⁱ
February	февраль	fevralʲ

March	март	mart
April	апрель	aprelʲ
May	май	maj
June	июнь	ijʉnʲ

July	июль	ijʉlʲ
August	август	avgust
September	сентябрь	sentʲabrʲ
October	октябрь	oktʲabrʲ
November	ноябрь	nojabrʲ
December	декабрь	dekabrʲ

spring	жаз	dʒaz
in spring	жазында	dʒazında
spring (as adj)	жазгы	dʒazgı

summer	жай	dʒaj
in summer	жайында	dʒajında
summer (as adj)	жайкы	dʒajkı

fall	күз	kyz
in fall	күзүндө	kyzyndø
fall (as adj)	күздүк	kyzdyk

winter	кыш	kıʃ
in winter	кышында	kıʃında
winter (as adj)	кышкы	kıʃkı

month	ай	aj
this month	ушул айда	uʃul ajda
next month	кийинки айда	kijinki ajda
last month	өткөн айда	øtkøn ajda

a month ago	бир ай мурун	bir aj murun
in a month (a month later)	бир айдан кийин	bir ajdan kijin
in 2 months (2 months later)	эки айдан кийин	eki ajdan kijin
the whole month	ай бою	aj bojʉ
all month long	толук бир ай	toluk bir aj

monthly (~ magazine)	ай сайын	aj sajın
monthly (adv)	ай сайын	aj sajın
every month	ар бир айда	ar bir ajda
twice a month	айына эки жолу	ajına eki dʒolu

year	жыл	dʒıl
this year	бул жылы	bul dʒılı
next year	келаткан жылы	kelatkan dʒılı
last year	өткөн жылы	øtkøn dʒılı

| a year ago | бир жыл мурун | bir dʒıl murun |
| in a year | бир жылдан кийин | bir dʒıldan kijin |

in two years	эки жылдан кийин	eki dʒıldan kijin
the whole year	жыл бою	dʒıl bodʒu
all year long	толук бир жыл	toluk bir dʒıl

every year	ар жыл сайын	ar dʒıl sajın
annual (adj)	жыл сайын	dʒıl sajın
annually (adv)	жыл сайын	dʒıl sajın
4 times a year	жылына төрт жолу	dʒılına tørt dʒolu

date (e.g., today's ~)	число	tʃislo
date (e.g., ~ of birth)	күн	kyn
calendar	календарь	kalendarʲ

half a year	жарым жыл	dʒarım dʒıl
six months	жарым чейрек	dʒarım tʃejrek
season (summer, etc.)	мезгил	mezgil
century	кылым	kılım

22. Units of measurement

weight	салмак	salmak
length	узундук	uzunduk
width	жазылык	dʒazılık
height	бийиктик	bijiktik
depth	терендик	tereŋdik
volume	көлөм	køløm
area	аянт	ajant

gram	грамм	gramm
milligram	миллиграмм	milligramm
kilogram	килограмм	kilogramm
ton	тонна	tonna
pound	фунт	funt
ounce	унция	untsija

meter	метр	metr
millimeter	миллиметр	millimetr
centimeter	сантиметр	santimetr
kilometer	километр	kilometr
mile	миля	milʲa

inch	дюйм	dujm
foot	фут	fut
yard	ярд	jard

| square meter | квадраттык метр | kvadrattık metr |
| hectare | гектар | gektar |

| liter | литр | litr |
| degree | градус | gradus |

volt	вольт	volʲt
ampere	ампер	amper
horsepower	ат күчү	at kytʃy

quantity	саны	sanı
a little bit of …	… бир аз	… bir az
half	жарым	dʒarım
dozen	он эки даана	on eki daana
piece (item)	даана	daana

| size | чоңдук | tʃoŋduk |
| scale (map ~) | өлчөмчен | øltʃømtʃen |

minimal (adj)	минималдуу	minimalduu
the smallest (adj)	эң кичинекей	eŋ kitʃinekej
medium (adj)	орточо	ortotʃo
maximal (adj)	максималдуу	maksimalduu
the largest (adj)	эң чоң	eŋ tʃoŋ

23. Containers

canning jar (glass ~)	банка	banka
can	банка	banka
bucket	чака	tʃaka
barrel	бочка	botʃka

wash basin (e.g., plastic ~)	дагара	dagara
tank (100L water ~)	бак	bak
hip flask	фляжка	flʲadʒka
jerrycan	канистра	kanistra
tank (e.g., tank car)	цистерна	tsısterna

mug	кружка	krudʒka
cup (of coffee, etc.)	чөйчөк	tʃøjtʃøk
saucer	табак	tabak
glass (tumbler)	ыстакан	ıstakan
wine glass	бокал	bokal
stock pot (soup pot)	мискей	miskej

| bottle (~ of wine) | бөтөлкө | bøtølkø |
| neck (of the bottle, etc.) | оозу | oozu |

carafe (decanter)	графин	grafin
pitcher	кумура	kumura
vessel (container)	идиш	idiʃ
pot (crock, stoneware ~)	карапа	karapa
vase	ваза	vaza

| flacon, bottle (perfume ~) | флакон | flakon |
| vial, small bottle | кичине бөтөлкө | kitʃine bøtølkø |

tube (of toothpaste)	тюбик	tʉbik
sack (bag)	кап	kap
bag (paper ~, plastic ~)	пакет	paket
pack (of cigarettes, etc.)	пачке	patʃke
box (e.g., shoebox)	куту	kutu
crate	үкөк	ykøk
basket	себет	sebet

HUMAN BEING

Human being. The body

24. Head

head	баш	baʃ
face	бет	bet
nose	мурун	murun
mouth	ооз	ooz
eye	көз	køz
eyes	көздөр	køzdør
pupil	карек	karek
eyebrow	каш	kaʃ
eyelash	кирпик	kirpik
eyelid	кабак	kabak
tongue	тил	til
tooth	тиш	tiʃ
lips	эриндер	erinder
cheekbones	бет сөөгү	bet søøgy
gum	тиш эти	tiʃ eti
palate	таңдай	taŋdaj
nostrils	мурун тешиги	murun teʃigi
chin	ээк	eek
jaw	жаак	dʒaak
cheek	бет	bet
forehead	чеке	tʃeke
temple	чыкый	tʃɪkɪj
ear	кулак	kulak
back of the head	желке	dʒelke
neck	моюн	mojʉn
throat	тамак	tamak
hair	чач	tʃatʃ
hairstyle	чач жасоо	tʃatʃ dʒasoo
haircut	чач кыркуу	tʃatʃ kɪrkuu
wig	парик	parik
mustache	мурут	murut
beard	сакал	sakal
to have (a beard, etc.)	мурут коюу	murut kojʉu

| braid | өрүм чач | ørym tʃatʃ |
| sideburns | бакенбарда | bakenbarda |

red-haired (adj)	сары	sarı
gray (hair)	ак чачтуу	ak tʃatʃtuu
bald (adj)	таз	taz
bald patch	кашка	kaʃka

| ponytail | куйрук | kujruk |
| bangs | көкүл | køkyl |

25. Human body

| hand | беш манжа | beʃ mandʒa |
| arm | кол | kol |

finger	манжа	mandʒa
toe	манжа	mandʒa
thumb	бармак	barmak
little finger	чыпалак	tʃıpalak
nail	тырмак	tırmak

fist	муштум	muʃtum
palm	алакан	alakan
wrist	билек	bilek
forearm	каруу	karuu
elbow	чыканак	tʃıkanak
shoulder	ийин	ijin

leg	бут	but
foot	таман	taman
knee	тизе	tize
calf (part of leg)	балтыр	baltır
hip	сан	san
heel	согончок	sogontʃok

body	дене	dene
stomach	курсак	kursak
chest	төш	tøʃ
breast	эмчек	emtʃek
flank	каптал	kaptal
back	арка жон	arka dʒon
lower back	бел	bel
waist	бел	bel
navel (belly button)	киндик	kindik
buttocks	жамбаш	dʒambaʃ
bottom	көчүк	køtʃyk
beauty mark	мең	meŋ
birthmark	кал	kal
(café au lait spot)		

| tattoo | татуировка | tatuirovka |
| scar | тырык | tırık |

Clothing & Accessories

26. Outerwear. Coats

clothes	кийим	kijim
outerwear	үстүнкү кийим	ystyŋky kijim
winter clothing	кышкы кийим	kɪʃkɪ kijim
coat (overcoat)	пальто	palʲto
fur coat	тон	ton
fur jacket	чолок тон	ʧolok ton
down coat	мамык олпок	mamɪk olpok
jacket (e.g., leather ~)	күрмө	kyrmø
raincoat (trenchcoat, etc.)	плащ	plaʃʧ
waterproof (adj)	суу өткүс	suu øtkys

27. Men's & women's clothing

shirt (button shirt)	көйнөк	køjnøk
pants	шым	ʃɪm
jeans	джинсы	ʤinsɪ
suit jacket	бешмант	beʃmant
suit	костюм	kostʉm
dress (frock)	көйнөк	køjnøk
skirt	юбка	jʉbka
blouse	блузка	bluzka
knitted jacket (cardigan, etc.)	кофта	kofta
jacket (of woman's suit)	кыска бешмант	kɪska beʃmant
T-shirt	футболка	futbolka
shorts (short trousers)	чолок шым	ʧolok ʃɪm
tracksuit	спорт кийими	sport kijimi
bathrobe	халат	χalat
pajamas	пижама	piʤama
sweater	свитер	sviter
pullover	пуловер	pulover
vest	жилет	ʤilet
tailcoat	фрак	frak
tuxedo	смокинг	smoking

uniform	форма	forma
workwear	жумуш кийим	dʒumuʃ kijim
overalls	комбинезон	kombinezon
coat (e.g., doctor's smock)	халат	χalat

28. Clothing. Underwear

underwear	ич кийим	itʃ kijim
boxers, briefs	эркектер чолок дамбалы	erkekter tʃolok dambalı
panties	аялдар трусиги	ajaldar trusigi
undershirt (A-shirt)	майка	majka
socks	байпак	bajpak

nightdress	жатаарда кийүүчү көйнөк	dʒataarda kijyytʃy køjnøk
bra	бюстгальтер	bʉstgalʲter
knee highs (knee-high socks)	гольфы	golʲfı
pantyhose	колготки	kolgotki
stockings (thigh highs)	байпак	bajpak
bathing suit	купальник	kupalʲnik

29. Headwear

| hat | топу | topu |
| fedora | шляпа | ʃlʲapa |

| baseball cap | бейсболка | bejsbolka |
| flatcap | кепка | kepka |

| beret | берет | beret |
| hood | капюшон | kapʉʃon |

| panama hat | панамка | panamka |
| knit cap (knitted hat) | токулган шапка | tokulgan ʃapka |

| headscarf | жоолук | dʒooluk |
| women's hat | шляпа | ʃlʲapa |

hard hat	каска	kaska
garrison cap	пилотка	pilotka
helmet	шлем	ʃlem

| derby | котелок | kotelok |
| top hat | цилиндр | tsılindr |

30. Footwear

footwear	бут кийим	but kijim
shoes (men's shoes)	ботинка	botinka
shoes (women's shoes)	туфли	tufli
boots (e.g., cowboy ~)	өтүк	øtyk
slippers	тапочка	tapotʃka
tennis shoes (e.g., Nike ~)	кроссовка	krossovka
sneakers (e.g., Converse ~)	кеды	kedı
sandals	сандалии	sandalii
cobbler (shoe repairer)	өтүкчү	øtyktʃy
heel	така	taka
pair (of shoes)	түгөй	tygøj
shoestring	боо	boo
to lace (vt)	боолоо	booloo
shoehorn	кашык	kaʃık
shoe polish	өтүк май	øtyk maj

31. Personal accessories

gloves	колкап	kolkap
mittens	мээлей	meelej
scarf (muffler)	моюн орогуч	mojʉn orogutʃ
glasses (eyeglasses)	көз айнек	køz ajnek
frame (eyeglass ~)	алкак	alkak
umbrella	чатырча	tʃatırtʃa
walking stick	аса таяк	asa tajak
hairbrush	тарак	tarak
fan	желпингич	dʒelpingitʃ
tie (necktie)	галстук	galstuk
bow tie	галстук-бабочка	galstuk-babotʃka
suspenders	шым тарткыч	ʃım tartkıtʃ
handkerchief	бетаарчы	betaartʃı
comb	тарак	tarak
barrette	чачсайгы	tʃatʃsajgı
hairpin	шпилька	ʃpilʲka
buckle	таралга	taralga
belt	кайыш кур	kajıʃ kur
shoulder strap	илгич	ilgitʃ
bag (handbag)	колбаштык	kolbaʃtık
purse	кичине колбаштык	kitʃine kolbaʃtık
backpack	жонбаштык	dʒonbaʃtık

32. Clothing. Miscellaneous

fashion	мода	moda
in vogue (adj)	саркеч	sarketʃ
fashion designer	модельер	modeljer
collar	жака	dʒaka
pocket	чөнтөк	tʃøntøk
pocket (as adj)	чөнтөк	tʃøntøk
sleeve	жең	dʒeŋ
hanging loop	илгич	ilgitʃ
fly (on trousers)	ширинка	ʃirinka
zipper (fastener)	молния	molnija
fastener	топчулук	toptʃuluk
button	топчу	toptʃu
buttonhole	илмек	ilmek
to come off (ab. button)	үзүлүү	yzylyy
to sew (vi, vt)	тигүү	tigyy
to embroider (vi, vt)	сайма саюу	sajma sajʉu
embroidery	сайма	sajma
sewing needle	ийне	ijne
thread	жип	dʒip
seam	тигиш	tigiʃ
to get dirty (vi)	булгап алуу	bulgap aluu
stain (mark, spot)	так	tak
to crease, crumple (vi)	бырышып калуу	bırıʃıp kaluu
to tear, to rip (vt)	айрылуу	ajrıluu
clothes moth	күбө	kybø

33. Personal care. Cosmetics

toothpaste	тиш пастасы	tiʃ pastası
toothbrush	тиш щёткасы	tiʃ ʃtʃʲotkası
to brush one's teeth	тиш жуу	tiʃ dʒuu
razor	устара	ustara
shaving cream	кырынуу үчүн көбүк	kırınuu ytʃyn købyk
to shave (vi)	кырынуу	kırınuu
soap	самын	samın
shampoo	шампунь	ʃampunʲ
scissors	кайчы	kajtʃı
nail file	тырмак өгөө	tırmak øgøø
nail clippers	тырмак кычкачы	tırmak kıtʃkatʃı
tweezers	искек	iskek

cosmetics	упа-эндик	upa-endik
face mask	маска	maska
manicure	маникюр	manik*r
to have a manicure	маникюр жасоо	manikʤ*r dʒasoo
pedicure	педикюр	pedik*r

make-up bag	косметичка	kosmetiʧka
face powder	упа	upa
powder compact	упа кутусу	upa kutusu
blusher	эндик	endik

perfume (bottled)	атыр	atır
toilet water (lotion)	туалет атыр суусу	tualet atır suusu
lotion	лосьон	losʲon
cologne	одеколон	odekolon

eyeshadow	көз боёгу	køz bojogu
eyeliner	көз карандашы	køz karandaʃı
mascara	кирпик үчүн боек	kirpik yʧyn boek

lipstick	эрин помадасы	erin pomadası
nail polish, enamel	тырмак үчүн лак	tırmak yʧyn lak
hair spray	чач үчүн лак	ʧaʧ yʧyn lak
deodorant	дезодорант	dezodorant

cream	крем	krem
face cream	бетмай	betmaj
hand cream	кол үчүн май	kol yʧyn maj
anti-wrinkle cream	бырыштарга каршы бет май	bırıʃtarga karʃı bet maj

day cream	күндүзгү бет май	kyndyzgy bet maj
night cream	түнкү бет май	tynky bet maj
day (as adj)	күндүзгү	kyndyzgy
night (as adj)	түнкү	tynky

tampon	тампон	tampon
toilet paper (toilet roll)	даарат кагазы	daarat kagazı
hair dryer	фен	fen

34. Watches. Clocks

watch (wristwatch)	кол саат	kol saat
dial	циферблат	ʦıferblat
hand (of clock, watch)	жебе	dʒebe
metal watch band	браслет	braslet
watch strap	кайыш кур	kajıʃ kur

battery	батарейка	batarejka
to be dead (battery)	зарядканын түгөнүүсү	zarʲadkanın tygønyysy
to change a battery	батарейка алмаштыруу	batarejka almaʃtıruu

| to run fast | алдыга кетүү | aldıga ketyy |
| to run slow | калуу | kaluu |

wall clock	дубалга тагуучу саат	dubalga taguuʧu saat
hourglass	кум саат	kum saat
sundial	күн саат	kyn saat
alarm clock	ойготкуч саат	ojgotkuʧ saat
watchmaker	саат устасы	saat ustası
to repair (vt)	оңдоо	oŋdoo

Food. Nutricion

35. Food

meat	эт	et
chicken	тоок	took
Rock Cornish hen (poussin)	балапан	balapan
duck	өрдөк	ørdøk
goose	каз	kaz
game	илбээсин	ilbeesin
turkey	күрп	kyrp
pork	чочко эти	tʃotʃko eti
veal	торпок эти	torpok eti
lamb	кой эти	koj eti
beef	уй эти	uj eti
rabbit	коен	koen
sausage (bologna, etc.)	колбаса	kolbasa
vienna sausage (frankfurter)	сосиска	sosiska
bacon	бекон	bekon
ham	ветчина	vettʃina
gammon	сан эт	san et
pâté	паштет	paʃtet
liver	боор	boor
hamburger (ground beef)	фарш	farʃ
tongue	тил	til
egg	жумуртка	dʒumurtka
eggs	жумурткалар	dʒumurtkalar
egg white	жумуртканын агы	dʒumurtkanın agı
egg yolk	жумуртканын сарысы	dʒumurtkanın sarısı
fish	балык	balık
seafood	деңиз азыктары	deŋiz azıktarı
crustaceans	рак сыяктуулар	rak sıjaktuular
caviar	урук	uruk
crab	краб	krab
shrimp	креветка	krevetka
oyster	устрица	ustritsa
spiny lobster	лангуст	langust
octopus	сегиз бут	segiz but

squid	кальмар	kalʲmar
sturgeon	осетрина	osetrina
salmon	лосось	lososʲ
halibut	палтус	paltus

cod	треска	treska
mackerel	скумбрия	skumbrija
tuna	тунец	tunets
eel	угорь	ugorʲ

trout	форель	forelʲ
sardine	сардина	sardina
pike	чортон	tʃorton
herring	сельдь	selʲdʲ

| bread | нан | nan |
| cheese | сыр | sır |

| sugar | кум шекер | kum-ʃeker |
| salt | туз | tuz |

rice	күрүч	kyrytʃ
pasta (macaroni)	макарон	makaron
noodles	кесме	kesme

| butter | ак май | ak maj |
| vegetable oil | өсүмдүк майы | øsymdyk majı |

| sunflower oil | күн карама майы | kyn karama majı |
| margarine | маргарин | margarin |

| olives | зайтун | zajtun |
| olive oil | зайтун майы | zajtun majı |

milk	сүт	syt
condensed milk	коютулган сүт	kojʉtulgan syt
yogurt	йогурт	jogurt

| sour cream | сметана | smetana |
| cream (of milk) | каймак | kajmak |

| mayonnaise | майонез | majonez |
| buttercream | крем | krem |

groats (barley ~, etc.)	акшак	akʃak
flour	ун	un
canned food	консерва	konserva

cornflakes	жарылган жүгөрү	dʒarılgan dʒygøry
honey	бал	bal
jam	джем, конфитюр	dʒem, konfitʉr
chewing gum	сагыз	sagız

36. Drinks

water	суу	suu
drinking water	ичүүчү суу	iʧyytʃy suu
mineral water	минерал суусу	mineral suusu

still (adj)	газсыз	gazsız
carbonated (adj)	газдалган	gazdalgan
sparkling (adj)	газы менен	gazı menen
ice	муз	muz
with ice	музу менен	muzu menen

non-alcoholic (adj)	алкоголсуз	alkogolsuz
soft drink	алкоголсуз ичимдик	alkogolsuz iʧimdik
refreshing drink	суусундук	suusunduk
lemonade	лимонад	limonad

liquors	спирт ичимдиктери	spirt iʧimdikteri
wine	шарап	ʃarap
white wine	ак шарап	ak ʃarap
red wine	кызыл шарап	kızıl ʃarap

liqueur	ликёр	likʲor
champagne	шампан	ʃampan
vermouth	вермут	vermut

whiskey	виски	viski
vodka	арак	arak
gin	джин	dʒin
cognac	коньяк	konjak
rum	ром	rom

coffee	кофе	kofe
black coffee	кара кофе	kara kofe
coffee with milk	сүттөлгөн кофе	syttølgøn kofe
cappuccino	капучино	kapuʧino
instant coffee	эрүүчү кофе	eryyʧy kofe

milk	сүт	syt
cocktail	коктейль	koktejlʲ
milkshake	сүт коктейли	syt koktejli

juice	шире	ʃire
tomato juice	томат ширеси	tomat ʃiresi
orange juice	апельсин ширеси	apelʲsin ʃiresi
freshly squeezed juice	түз сыгылып алынган шире	tyz sıgılıp alıngan ʃire

beer	сыра	sıra
light beer	ачык сыра	atʃık sıra
dark beer	коңур сыра	koŋur sıra

tea	чай	ʧaj
black tea	кара чай	kara ʧaj
green tea	жашыл чай	ʤaʃɪl ʧaj

37. Vegetables

| vegetables | жашылча | ʤaʃɪlʧa |
| greens | көк чөп | køk ʧøp |

tomato	помидор	pomidor
cucumber	бадыраң	badɪraŋ
carrot	сабиз	sabiz
potato	картошка	kartoʃka
onion	пияз	pijaz
garlic	сарымсак	sarɪmsak

cabbage	капуста	kapusta
cauliflower	гүлдүү капуста	gyldyy kapusta
Brussels sprouts	брюссель капустасы	brʉselʲ kapustasɪ
broccoli	брокколи капустасы	brokkoli kapustasɪ

beet	кызылча	kɪzɪlʧa
eggplant	баклажан	baklaʤan
zucchini	кабачок	kabatʃok
pumpkin	ашкабак	aʃkabak
turnip	шалгам	ʃalgam

parsley	петрушка	petruʃka
dill	укроп	ukrop
lettuce	салат	salat
celery	сельдерей	selʲderej
asparagus	спаржа	spardʒa
spinach	шпинат	ʃpinat

pea	нокот	nokot
beans	буурчак	buurʧak
corn (maize)	жүгөрү	ʤygøry
kidney bean	төө буурчак	tøø buurʧak

bell pepper	таттуу перец	tattuu perets
radish	шалгам	ʃalgam
artichoke	артишок	artiʃok

38. Fruits. Nuts

fruit	мөмө	mømø
apple	алма	alma
pear	алмурут	almurut

lemon	лимон	limon
orange	апельсин	apelʲsin
strawberry (garden ~)	кулпунай	kulpunaj

mandarin	мандарин	mandarin
plum	кара өрүк	kara øryk
peach	шабдаалы	ʃabdaalı
apricot	өрүк	øryk
raspberry	дан куурай	dan kuuraj
pineapple	ананас	ananas

banana	банан	banan
watermelon	арбуз	arbuz
grape	жүзүм	dʒyzym
sour cherry	алча	alʧa
sweet cherry	гилас	gilas
melon	коон	koon

grapefruit	грейпфрут	grejpfrut
avocado	авокадо	avokado
papaya	папайя	papaja
mango	манго	mango
pomegranate	анар	anar

redcurrant	кызыл карагат	kızıl karagat
blackcurrant	кара карагат	kara karagat
gooseberry	крыжовник	krıdʒovnik
bilberry	кара моюл	kara mojʉl
blackberry	кара бүлдүркөн	kara byldyrkøn

raisin	мейиз	mejiz
fig	анжир	andʒir
date	курма	kurma

peanut	арахис	araχis
almond	бадам	badam
walnut	жаңгак	dʒaŋgak
hazelnut	токой жаңгагы	tokoj dʒaŋgagı
coconut	кокос жаңгагы	kokos dʒaŋgagı
pistachios	мисте	miste

39. Bread. Candy

bakers' confectionery (pastry)	кондитер азыктары	konditer azıktarı
bread	нан	nan
cookies	печенье	petʃenje

| chocolate (n) | шоколад | ʃokolad |
| chocolate (as adj) | шоколаддан | ʃokoladdan |

candy (wrapped)	конфета	konfeta
cake (e.g., cupcake)	пирожное	pirodʒnoe
cake (e.g., birthday ~)	торт	tort
pie (e.g., apple ~)	пирог	pirog
filling (for cake, pie)	начинка	natʃinka
jam (whole fruit jam)	кыям	kıjam
marmalade	мармелад	marmelad
wafers	вафли	vafli
ice-cream	бал муздак	bal muzdak
pudding	пудинг	puding

40. Cooked dishes

course, dish	тамак	tamak
cuisine	даам	daam
recipe	тамак жасоо ыкмасы	tamak dʒasoo ıkması
portion	порция	portsija
salad	салат	salat
soup	сорпо	sorpo
clear soup (broth)	ынак сорпо	ınak sorpo
sandwich (bread)	бутерброд	buterbrod
fried eggs	куурулган жумуртка	kuurulgan dʒumurtka
hamburger (beefburger)	гамбургер	gamburger
beefsteak	бифштекс	bifʃteks
side dish	гарнир	garnir
spaghetti	спагетти	spagetti
mashed potatoes	эзилген картошка	ezilgen kartoʃka
pizza	пицца	pitsa
porridge (oatmeal, etc.)	ботко	botko
omelet	омлет	omlet
boiled (e.g., ~ beef)	сууга бышырылган	suuga bıʃırılgan
smoked (adj)	ышталган	ıʃtalgan
fried (adj)	куурулган	kuurulgan
dried (adj)	кургатылган	kurgatılgan
frozen (adj)	тондурулган	toŋdurulgan
pickled (adj)	маринаддагы	marinaddagı
sweet (sugary)	таттуу	tattuu
salty (adj)	туздуу	tuzduu
cold (adj)	муздак	muzdak
hot (adj)	ысык	ısık
bitter (adj)	ачуу	atʃuu
tasty (adj)	daamduu	daamduu

to cook in boiling water	кайнатуу	kajnatuu
to cook (dinner)	тамак бышыруу	tamak bıʃıruu
to fry (vt)	кууруу	kuuruu
to heat up (food)	жылытуу	dʒılıtuu

to salt (vt)	туздоо	tuzdoo
to pepper (vt)	калемпир кошуу	kalempir koʃuu
to grate (vt)	сүргүлөө	syrgyløø
peel (n)	сырты	sırtı
to peel (vt)	тазалоо	tazaloo

41. Spices

salt	туз	tuz
salty (adj)	туздуу	tuzduu
to salt (vt)	туздоо	tuzdoo

black pepper	кара мурч	kara murtʃ
red pepper (milled ~)	кызыл калемпир	kızıl kalempir
mustard	горчица	gortʃitsa
horseradish	хрен	χren

condiment	татымал	tatımal
spice	татымал	tatımal
sauce	соус	sous
vinegar	уксус	uksus

anise	анис	anis
basil	райхон	rajχon
cloves	гвоздика	gvozdika
ginger	имбирь	imbirʲ
coriander	кориандр	koriandr
cinnamon	корица	koritsa

sesame	кунжут	kundʒut
bay leaf	лавр жалбырагы	lavr dʒalbıragı
paprika	паприка	paprika
caraway	зира	zira
saffron	заапаран	zaaparan

42. Meals

| food | тамак | tamak |
| to eat (vi, vt) | тамактануу | tamaktanuu |

| breakfast | таңкы тамак | taŋkı tamak |
| to have breakfast | эртең менен тамактануу | erteŋ menen tamaktanuu |

lunch	түшкү тамак	tyʃky tamak
to have lunch	түштөнүү	tyʃtønyy
dinner	кечки тамак	ketʃki tamak
to have dinner	кечки тамакты ичүү	ketʃki tamaktı itʃyy

| appetite | табит | tabit |
| Enjoy your meal! | Тамагыңыз таттуу болсун! | tamagıŋız tattuu bolsun! |

to open (~ a bottle)	ачуу	atʃuu
to spill (liquid)	төгүп алуу	tøgyp aluu
to spill out (vi)	төгүлүү	tøgylyy

to boil (vi)	кайноо	kajnoo
to boil (vt)	кайнатуу	kajnatuu
boiled (~ water)	кайнатылган	kajnatılgan
to chill, cool down (vt)	суутуу	suutuu
to chill (vi)	сууп туруу	suup turuu

| taste, flavor | даам | daam |
| aftertaste | даамдануу | daamdanuu |

to slim down (lose weight)	арыктоо	arıktoo
diet	мүнөз тамак	mynøz tamak
vitamin	витамин	vitamin
calorie	калория	kalorija
vegetarian (n)	эттен чанган	etten tʃangan
vegetarian (adj)	этсиз даярдалган	etsiz dajardalgan

fats (nutrient)	майлар	majlar
proteins	белоктор	beloktor
carbohydrates	көмүрсуулар	kømyrsuular

slice (of lemon, ham)	кесим	kesim
piece (of cake, pie)	бөлүк	bølyk
crumb (of bread, cake, etc.)	күкүм	kykym

43. Table setting

spoon	кашык	kaʃik
knife	бычак	bıtʃak
fork	вилка	vilka

| cup (e.g., coffee ~) | чөйчөк | tʃøjtʃøk |
| plate (dinner ~) | табак | tabak |

saucer	табак	tabak
napkin (on table)	майлык	majlık
toothpick	тиш чукугуч	tiʃ tʃukugutʃ

44. Restaurant

restaurant	ресторан	restoran
coffee house	кофекана	kofekana
pub, bar	бар	bar
tearoom	чай салону	ʧaj salonu
waiter	официант	ofiʦiant
waitress	официант кыз	ofiʦiant kız
bartender	бармен	barmen
menu	меню	menu
wine list	шарап картасы	ʃarap kartası
to book a table	столду камдык буйрутмалоо	stoldu kamdık bujrutmaloo
course, dish	тамак	tamak
to order (meal)	буйрутма кылуу	bujrutma kıluu
to make an order	буйрутма берүү	bujrutma beryy
aperitif	аперитив	aperitiv
appetizer	ысылык	ısılık
dessert	десерт	desert
check	эсеп	esep
to pay the check	эсеп төлөө	esep tøløø
to give change	майда акчаны кайтаруу	majda akʧanı kajtaruu
tip	чайпул	ʧajpul

Family, relatives and friends

45. Personal information. Forms

name (first name)	**аты**	atı
surname (last name)	**фамилиясы**	familijası
date of birth	**төрөлгөн күнү**	tørølgøn kyny
place of birth	**туулган жери**	tuulgan dʒeri
nationality	**улуту**	ulutu
place of residence	**жашаган жери**	dʒaʃagan dʒeri
country	**өлкө**	ølkø
profession (occupation)	**кесиби**	kesibi
gender, sex	**жынысы**	dʒınısı
height	**бою**	bojʉ
weight	**салмак**	salmak

46. Family members. Relatives

mother	**эне**	ene
father	**ата**	ata
son	**уул**	uul
daughter	**кыз**	kız
younger daughter	**кичүү кыз**	kitʃyy kız
younger son	**кичүү уул**	kitʃyy uul
eldest daughter	**улуу кыз**	uluu kız
eldest son	**улуу уул**	uluu uul
brother	**бир тууган**	bir tuugan
elder brother	**байке**	bajke
younger brother	**ини**	ini
sister	**бир тууган**	bir tuugan
elder sister	**эже**	edʒe
younger sister	**синди**	siŋdi
cousin (masc.)	**атасы же энеси**	atası dʒe enesi
	бир тууган	bir tuugan
cousin (fem.)	**атасы же энеси**	atası dʒe enesi
	бир тууган	bir tuugan
mom, mommy	**апа**	apa
dad, daddy	**ата**	ata

parents	ата-эне	ata-ene
child	бала	bala
children	балдар	baldar

grandmother	чоӊ апа	tʃoŋ apa
grandfather	чоӊ ата	tʃoŋ ata
grandson	небере бала	nebere bala
granddaughter	небере кыз	nebere kız
grandchildren	неберелер	nebereler

uncle	таяке	tajake
aunt	таяже	tajadʒe
nephew	ини	ini
niece	жээн	dʒeen

mother-in-law (wife's mother)	кайын эне	kajın ene
father-in-law (husband's father)	кайын ата	kajın ata
son-in-law (daughter's husband)	күйөө бала	kyjøø bala
stepmother	өгөй эне	øgøj ene
stepfather	өгөй ата	øgøj ata

infant	эмчектеги бала	emtʃektegi bala
baby (infant)	ымыркай	ımırkaj
little boy, kid	бөбөк	bøbøk

wife	аял	ajal
husband	эр	er
spouse (husband)	күйөө	kyjøø
spouse (wife)	зайып	zajıp

married (masc.)	аялы бар	ajalı bar
married (fem.)	күйөөдө	kyjøødø
single (unmarried)	бойдок	bojdok
bachelor	бойдок	bojdok
divorced (masc.)	ажырашкан	adʒıraʃkan
widow	жесир	dʒesir
widower	жесир	dʒesir

relative	тууган	tuugan
close relative	жакын тууган	dʒakın tuugan
distant relative	алыс тууган	alıs tuugan
relatives	бир тууган	bir tuugan

orphan (boy or girl)	жетим	dʒetim
guardian (of a minor)	камкорчу	kamkortʃu
to adopt (a boy)	уул кылып асырап алуу	uul kılıp asırap aluu
to adopt (a girl)	кыз кылып асырап алуу	kız kılıp asırap aluu

Medicine

47. Diseases

sickness	оору	ooru
to be sick	ооруу	ooruu
health	ден-соолук	den-sooluk
runny nose (coryza)	мурдунан суу агуу	murdunan suu aguu
tonsillitis	ангина	angina
cold (illness)	суук тийүү	suuk tijyy
to catch a cold	суук тийгизип алуу	suuk tijgizip aluu
bronchitis	бронхит	bronхit
pneumonia	кабыргадан сезгенүү	kabırgadan sezgenyy
flu, influenza	сасык тумоо	sasık tumoo
nearsighted (adj)	алыстан көрө албоо	alıstan kørø alboo
farsighted (adj)	жакындан көрө албоо	dʒakından kørø alboo
strabismus (crossed eyes)	кылый көздүүлүк	kılıj køzdyylyk
cross-eyed (adj)	кылый көздүүлүк	kılıj køzdyylyk
cataract	челкөз	tʃelkøz
glaucoma	глаукома	glaukoma
stroke	мээге кан куюлуу	meege kan kujuluu
heart attack	инфаркт	infarkt
myocardial infarction	инфаркт миокарда	infarkt miokarda
paralysis	шал	ʃal
to paralyze (vt)	шал болуу	ʃal boluu
allergy	аллергия	allergija
asthma	астма	astma
diabetes	диабет	diabet
toothache	тиш оорусу	tiʃ oorusu
caries	кариес	karies
diarrhea	ич өткү	itʃ øtky
constipation	ич катуу	itʃ katuu
stomach upset	ич бузулгандык	itʃ buzulgandık
food poisoning	уулануу	uulanuu
to get food poisoning	уулануу	uulanuu
arthritis	артрит	artrit
rickets	итий	itij
rheumatism	кызыл жүгүрүк	kızıl dʒygyryk

atherosclerosis	атеросклероз	ateroskleroz
gastritis	карын сезгенүүсу	karın sezgenyysu
appendicitis	аппендицит	appenditsit
cholecystitis	холецистит	χoletsistit
ulcer	жара	dʒara

measles	кызылча	kızıltʃa
rubella (German measles)	кызамык	kızamık
jaundice	сарык	sarık
hepatitis	гепатит	gepatit

schizophrenia	шизофрения	ʃizofrenija
rabies (hydrophobia)	кутурма	kuturma
neurosis	невроз	nevroz
concussion	мээнин чайкалышы	meenin tʃajkalıʃı

cancer	рак	rak
sclerosis	склероз	skleroz
multiple sclerosis	жайылган склероз	dʒajılgan skleroz

alcoholism	аракечтик	araketʃtik
alcoholic (n)	аракеч	araketʃ
syphilis	котон жара	koton dʒara
AIDS	СПИД	spid

tumor	шишик	ʃiʃik
malignant (adj)	залалдуу	zalalduu
benign (adj)	залалсыз	zalalsız

fever	безгек	bezgek
malaria	безгек	bezgek
gangrene	кабыз	kabız
seasickness	деңиз оорусу	deŋiz oorusu
epilepsy	талма	talma

epidemic	эпидемия	epidemija
typhus	келте	kelte
tuberculosis	кургак учук	kurgak utʃuk
cholera	холера	χolera
plague (bubonic ~)	кара тумоо	kara tumoo

48. Symptoms. Treatments. Part 1

symptom	белги	belgi
temperature	дене табынын көтөрүлүшу	dene tabının køtørylyʃy
high temperature (fever)	жогорку температура	dʒogorku temperatura
pulse (heartbeat)	тамыр кагышы	tamır kagıʃı
dizziness (vertigo)	баш айлануу	baʃ ajlanuu
hot (adj)	ысык	ısık

shivering	чыйрыгуу	tʃijrɪguu
pale (e.g., ~ face)	купкуу	kupkuu

cough	жөтөл	dʒøtøl
to cough (vi)	жөтөлүү	dʒøtølyy
to sneeze (vi)	чүчкүрүү	tʃytʃkyryy
faint	эси оо	esi oo
to faint (vi)	эси ооп жыгылуу	esi oop dʒɪgɪluu

bruise (hématome)	көк-ала	køk-ala
bump (lump)	шишик	ʃiʃik
to bang (bump)	урунуп алуу	urunup aluu
contusion (bruise)	көгөртүп алуу	køgørtyp aluu
to get a bruise	көгөртүп алуу	køgørtyp aluu

to limp (vi)	аксоо	aksoo
dislocation	муундун чыгып кетүүсү	muundun tʃɪgɪp ketyysy
to dislocate (vt)	чыгарып алуу	tʃɪgarɪp aluu
fracture	сынуу	sɪnuu
to have a fracture	сындырып алуу	sɪndɪrɪp aluu

cut (e.g., paper ~)	кесилген жер	kesilgen dʒer
to cut oneself	кесип алуу	kesip aluu
bleeding	кан кетүү	kan ketyy

burn (injury)	күйүк	kyjyk
to get burned	күйгүзүп алуу	kyjgyzyp aluu

to prick (vt)	саюу	sajɵu
to prick oneself	сайып алуу	sajɪp aluu
to injure (vt)	кокустатып алуу	kokustatɪp aluu
injury	кокустатып алуу	kokustatɪp aluu
wound	жара	dʒara
trauma	жаракат	dʒarakat

to be delirious	жөлүү	dʒølyy
to stutter (vi)	кекечтенүү	keketʃtenyy
sunstroke	күн өтүү	kyn øtyy

49. Symptoms. Treatments. Part 2

pain, ache	оору	ooru
splinter (in foot, etc.)	тикен	tiken

sweat (perspiration)	тер	ter
to sweat (perspire)	тердөө	terdøø
vomiting	кусуу	kusuu
convulsions	тарамыш карышуусу	taramɪʃ karɪʃuusu
pregnant (adj)	кош бойлуу	koʃ bojluu
to be born	төрөлүү	tørølyy

delivery, labor	төрөт	tørøt
to deliver (~ a baby)	төрөө	tørøø
abortion	бойдон түшүрүү	bojdon tyʃyryy
breathing, respiration	дем алуу	dem aluu
in-breath (inhalation)	дем алуу	dem aluu
out-breath (exhalation)	дем чыгаруу	dem ʧɪgaruu
to exhale (breathe out)	дем чыгаруу	dem ʧɪgaruu
to inhale (vi)	дем алуу	dem aluu
disabled person	майып	majɪp
cripple	мунжу	mundʒu
drug addict	баңги	baŋgi
deaf (adj)	дүлөй	dyløj
mute (adj)	дудук	duduk
deaf mute (adj)	дудук	duduk
mad, insane (adj)	жин тийген	dʒin tijgen
madman (demented person)	жинди чалыш	dʒindi ʧalɪʃ
madwoman	жинди чалыш	dʒindi ʧalɪʃ
to go insane	мээси айныган	meesi ajnɪgan
gene	ген	gen
immunity	иммунитет	immunitet
hereditary (adj)	тукум куучулук	tukum kuuʧuluk
congenital (adj)	тубаса	tubasa
virus	вирус	virus
microbe	микроб	mikrob
bacterium	бактерия	bakterija
infection	жугуштуу илдет	dʒuguʃtuu ildet

50. Symptoms. Treatments. Part 3

hospital	оорукана	oorukana
patient	бейтап	bejtap
diagnosis	дарт аныктоо	dart anɪktoo
cure	дарылоо	darɪloo
medical treatment	дарылоо	darɪloo
to get treatment	дарылануу	darɪlanuu
to treat (~ a patient)	дарылоо	darɪloo
to nurse (look after)	кароо	karoo
care (nursing ~)	кароо	karoo
operation, surgery	операция	operatsija
to bandage (head, limb)	жараны таңуу	dʒaranɪ taŋuu
bandaging	таңуу	taŋuu

vaccination	эмдөө	emdøø
to vaccinate (vt)	эмдөө	emdøø
injection, shot	ийне салуу	ijne saluu
to give an injection	ийне сайдыруу	ijne sajdıruu

attack	оору кармап калуу	ooru karmap kaluu
amputation	кесүү	kesyy
to amputate (vt)	кесип таштоо	kesip taʃtoo
coma	кома	koma
to be in a coma	комада болуу	komada boluu
intensive care	реанимация	reanimatsija

to recover (~ from flu)	сакаюу	sakajɥu
condition (patient's ~)	абал	abal
consciousness	эсинде	esinde
memory (faculty)	эс тутум	es tutum

to pull out (tooth)	тишти жулуу	tiʃti ʤuluu
filling	пломба	plomba
to fill (a tooth)	пломба салуу	plomba saluu

| hypnosis | гипноз | gipnoz |
| to hypnotize (vt) | гипноз кылуу | gipnoz kıluu |

51. Doctors

doctor	доктур	doktur
nurse	медсестра	medsestra
personal doctor	жекелик доктур	ʤekelik doktur

dentist	тиш доктур	tiʃ doktur
eye doctor	көз доктур	køz doktur
internist	терапевт	terapevt
surgeon	хирург	χirurg

psychiatrist	психиатр	psiχiatr
pediatrician	педиатр	pediatr
psychologist	психолог	psiχolog
gynecologist	гинеколог	ginekolog
cardiologist	кардиолог	kardiolog

52. Medicine. Drugs. Accessories

medicine, drug	дары-дармек	darı-darmek
remedy	дары	darı
to prescribe (vt)	жазып берүү	ʤazıp beryy
prescription	рецепт	reʦept
tablet, pill	таблетка	tabletka

ointment	май	maj
ampule	ампула	ampula
mixture, solution	аралашма	aralaʃma
syrup	сироп	sirop
capsule	пилюля	piluⁱlⁱa
powder	күкүм	kykym

gauze bandage	бинт	bint
cotton wool	пахта	paχta
iodine	йод	jod

Band-Aid	лейкопластырь	lejkoplastırⁱ
eyedropper	дары тамызгыч	darı tamızgıʧ
thermometer	градусник	gradusnik
syringe	шприц	ʃprits

| wheelchair | майып арабасы | majıp arabası |
| crutches | колтук таяк | koltuk tajak |

painkiller	оору сездирбөөчү дары	ooru sezdirbøøʧy darı
laxative	ич алдыруучу дары	iʧ aldıruuʧu darı
spirits (ethanol)	спирт	spirt
medicinal herbs	дары чөптөр	darı ʧøptør
herbal (~ tea)	чөп чайы	ʧøp ʧajı

HUMAN HABITAT

City

53. City. Life in the city

city, town	шаар	ʃaar
capital city	борбор	borbor
village	кыштак	kıʃtak
city map	шаардын планы	ʃaardın planı
downtown	шаардын борбору	ʃaardın borboru
suburb	шаардын чет жакасы	ʃaardın tʃet dʒakası
suburban (adj)	шаардын чет жакасындагы	ʃaardın tʃet dʒakasındagı
outskirts	чет-жака	tʃet-dʒaka
environs (suburbs)	чет-жака	tʃet-dʒaka
city block	квартал	kvartal
residential block (area)	турак-жай кварталы	turak-dʒaj kvartalı
traffic	көчө кыймылы	køtʃø kıjmılı
traffic lights	светофор	svetofor
public transportation	шаар транспорту	ʃaar transportu
intersection	кесилиш	kesiliʃ
crosswalk	жөө жүрүүчүлөр жолу	dʒøø dʒyryytʃylør dʒolu
pedestrian underpass	жер астындагы жол	dʒer astındagı dʒol
to cross (~ the street)	жолду өтүү	dʒoldu øtyy
pedestrian	жөө жүрүүчү	dʒøø dʒyryytʃy
sidewalk	жанжол	dʒandʒol
bridge	көпүрө	køpyrø
embankment (river walk)	жээк жол	dʒeek dʒol
fountain	фонтан	fontan
allée (garden walkway)	аллея	alleja
park	сейил багы	sejil bagı
boulevard	бульвар	bulʲvar
square	аянт	ajant
avenue (wide street)	проспект	prospekt
street	көчө	køtʃø
side street	чолок көчө	tʃolok køtʃø
dead end	туюк көчө	tujuk køtʃø
house	үй	yj

building	имарат	imarat
skyscraper	көк тиреген көп кабаттуу үй	køk tiregen køp kabattuu yj

facade	үйдүн алды	yjdyn aldı
roof	чатыр	tʃatır
window	терезе	tereze
arch	түркүк	tyrkyk
column	мамы	mamı
corner	бурч	burtʃ

store window	көрсөтмө айнек үкөк	kørsøtmø ajnek ykøk
signboard (store sign, etc.)	көрнөк	kørnøk
poster (e.g., playbill)	афиша	afiʃa
advertising poster	көрнөк-жарнак	kørnøk-dʒarnak
billboard	жарнамалык такта	dʒarnamalık takta

garbage, trash	таштанды	taʃtandı
trash can (public ~)	таштанды челек	taʃtandı tʃelek
to litter (vi)	таштоо	taʃtoo
garbage dump	таштанды үйүлгөн жер	taʃtandı yjylgøn dʒer

phone booth	телефон будкасы	telefon budkası
lamppost	чырак мамы	tʃırak mamı
bench (park ~)	отургуч	oturgutʃ

police officer	полиция кызматкери	politsija kızmatkeri
police	полиция	politsija
beggar	кайырчы	kajırtʃı
homeless (n)	селсаяк	selsajak

54. Urban institutions

store	дүкөн	dykøn
drugstore, pharmacy	дарыкана	darıkana
eyeglass store	оптика	optika
shopping mall	соода борбору	sooda borboru
supermarket	супермаркет	supermarket

bakery	нан дүкөнү	nan dykøny
baker	навайчы	navajtʃı
pastry shop	кондитердик дүкөн	konditerdik dykøn
grocery store	азык-түлүк	azık-tylyk
butcher shop	эт дүкөнү	et dykøny

produce store	жашылча дүкөнү	dʒaʃıltʃa dykøny
market	базар	bazar

coffee house	кофекана	kofekana
restaurant	ресторан	restoran

| pub, bar | сыракана | sırakana |
| pizzeria | пиццерия | pitserija |

hair salon	чач тарач	tʃatʃ taratʃ
post office	почта	potʃta
dry cleaners	химиялык тазалоо	χimijalık tazaloo
photo studio	фотоателье	fotoatelje

shoe store	бут кийим дүкөнү	but kijim dykøny
bookstore	китеп дүкөнү	kitep dykøny
sporting goods store	спорт буюмдар дүкөнү	sport bujumdar dykøny

clothes repair shop	кийим ондоочу жай	kijim ondootʃu dʒaj
formal wear rental	кийимди ижарага берүү	kijimdi idʒaraga beryy
video rental store	тасмаларды ижарага берүү	tasmalardı idʒaraga beryy

circus	цирк	tsırk
zoo	зоопарк	zoopark
movie theater	кинотеатр	kinoteatr
museum	музей	muzej
library	китепкана	kitepkana

theater	театр	teatr
opera (opera house)	опера	opera
nightclub	түнкү клуб	tynky klub
casino	казино	kazino

mosque	мечит	metʃit
synagogue	синагога	sinagoga
cathedral	чоң чиркөө	tʃoŋ tʃirkøø
temple	ибадаткана	ibadatkana
church	чиркөө	tʃirkøø

college	коллеж	kolledʒ
university	университет	universitet
school	мектеп	mektep

prefecture	префектура	prefektura
city hall	мэрия	merija
hotel	мейманкана	mejmankana
bank	банк	bank

embassy	элчилик	eltʃilik
travel agency	турагенттиги	turagenttigi
information office	маалымат бюросу	maalımat burosu
currency exchange	алмаштыруу пункту	almaʃtıruu punktu

subway	метро	metro
hospital	оорукана	oorukana
gas station	май куюучу станция	maj kujuutʃu stantsija
parking lot	унаа токтоочу жай	unaa toktootʃu dʒaj

55. Signs

signboard (store sign, etc.)	көрнөк	kørnøk
notice (door sign, etc.)	жазуу	dʒazuu
poster	көрнөк	kørnøk
direction sign	көрсөткүч	kørsøtkytʃ
arrow (sign)	жебе	dʒebe
caution	экертме	ekertme
warning sign	эскертүү белгиси	eskertyy belgisi
to warn (vt)	эскертүү	eskertyy
rest day (weekly ~)	дем алыш күн	dem alıʃ kyn
timetable (schedule)	ырааттама	ıraattama
opening hours	иш сааттары	iʃ saattarı
WELCOME!	КОШ КЕЛИҢИЗДЕР!	koʃ keliŋizder!
ENTRANCE	КИРҮҮ	kiryy
EXIT	ЧЫГУУ	tʃıguu
PUSH	ӨЗҮҢҮЗДӨН ТҮРТҮҢҮЗ	øzyŋyzdøn tyrtyŋyz
PULL	ӨЗҮҢҮЗГӨ ТАРТЫҢЫЗ	øzyŋyzgø tartıŋız
OPEN	АЧЫК	atʃık
CLOSED	ЖАБЫК	dʒabık
WOMEN	АЙЫМДАР ҮЧҮН	ajımdar ytʃyn
MEN	ЭРКЕКТЕР ҮЧҮН	erkekter ytʃyn
DISCOUNTS	АРЗАНДАТУУЛАР	arzandatuular
SALE	САТЫП ТҮГӨТҮҮ	satıp tygøtyy
NEW!	СААМАЛЫК!	saamalık!
FREE	БЕКЕР	beker
ATTENTION!	КӨҢҮЛ БУРУҢУЗ!	køŋyl buruŋuz!
NO VACANCIES	ОРУН ЖОК	orun dʒok
RESERVED	КАМДЫК БУЙРУТМАЛАГАН	kamdık bujrutmalagan
ADMINISTRATION	АДМИНИСТРАЦИЯ	administratsija
STAFF ONLY	ЖААМАТ ҮЧҮН ГАНА	dʒaamat ytʃyn gana
BEWARE OF THE DOG!	КАБАНААК ИТ	kabanaak it
NO SMOKING	ТАМЕКИ ЧЕГҮҮГӨ БОЛБОЙТ!	tameki tʃegyygø bolbojt!
DO NOT TOUCH!	КОЛУҢАР МЕНЕН КАРМАБАГЫЛА!	koluŋar menen karmabagıla!
DANGEROUS	КООПТУУ	kooptuu
DANGER	КОРКУНУЧ	korkunutʃ
HIGH VOLTAGE	ЖОГОРКУ ЧЫҢАЛУУ	dʒogorku tʃıŋaluu
NO SWIMMING!	СУУГА ТҮШҮҮГӨ БОЛБОЙТ	suuga tyʃyygø bolbojt

OUT OF ORDER	ИШТЕБЕЙТ	iʃtebejt
FLAMMABLE	ӨРТ ЧЫГУУ	ørt tʃɪguu
	КОРКУНУЧУ	korkunutʃu
FORBIDDEN	ТЫЮУ САЛЫНГАН	tɪjʉu salɪngan
NO TRESPASSING!	ӨТҮҮГӨ БОЛБОЙТ	øtyygø bolbojt
WET PAINT	СЫРДАЛГАН	sɪrdalgan

56. Urban transportation

bus	автобус	avtobus
streetcar	трамвай	tramvaj
trolley bus	троллейбус	trollejbus
route (of bus, etc.)	каттам	kattam
number (e.g., bus ~)	номер	nomer

to go by ...	... жүрүү	... dʒyryy
to get on (~ the bus)	... отуруу	... oturuu
to get off ...	... түшүп калуу	... tyʃyp kaluu

stop (e.g., bus ~)	аялдама	ajaldama
next stop	кийинки аялдама	kijinki ajaldama
terminus	акыркы аялдама	akɪrkɪ ajaldama
schedule	ырааттама	ɪraattama
to wait (vt)	күтүү	kytyy

| ticket | билет | bilet |
| fare | билеттин баасы | bilettin baasɪ |

cashier (ticket seller)	кассир	kassir
ticket inspection	текшерүү	tekʃeryy
ticket inspector	текшерүүчү	tekʃeryytʃy

to be late (for ...)	кечигүү	ketʃigyy
to miss (~ the train, etc.)	кечигип калуу	ketʃigip kaluu
to be in a hurry	шашуу	ʃaʃuu

taxi, cab	такси	taksi
taxi driver	такси айдоочу	taksi ajdootʃu
by taxi	таксиде	takside
taxi stand	такси токтоочу жай	taksi toktootʃu dʒaj
to call a taxi	такси чакыруу	taksi tʃakɪruu
to take a taxi	такси кармоо	taksi karmoo

traffic	көчө кыймылы	køtʃø kɪjmɪlɪ
traffic jam	тыгын	tɪgɪn
rush hour	кызуу маал	kɪzuu maal
to park (vi)	токтотуу	toktotuu
to park (vt)	машинаны	maʃinanɪ
	жайлаштыруу	dʒajlaʃtɪruu

| parking lot | унаа токтоочу жай | unaa toktootʃu dʒaj |

subway	метро	metro
station	бекет	beket
to take the subway	метродо жүрүү	metrodo dӡyryy
train	поезд	poezd
train station	вокзал	vokzal

57. Sightseeing

monument	эстелик	estelik
fortress	чеп	ʧep
palace	сарай	saraj
castle	сепил	sepil
tower	мунара	munara
mausoleum	күмбөз	kymbøz

architecture	архитектура	arχitektura
medieval (adj)	орто кылымдык	orto kılımdık
ancient (adj)	байыркы	bajırkı
national (adj)	улуттук	uluttuk
famous (monument, etc.)	таанымал	taanımal

tourist	турист	turist
guide (person)	гид	gid
excursion, sightseeing tour	экскурсия	ekskursija
to show (vt)	көрсөтүү	kørsøtyy
to tell (vt)	айтып берүү	ajtıp beryy

to find (vt)	табуу	tabuu
to get lost (lose one's way)	адашып кетүү	adaʃıp ketyy
map (e.g., subway ~)	схема	sχema
map (e.g., city ~)	план	plan

souvenir, gift	асембелек	asembelek
gift shop	асембелек дүкөнү	asembelek dykøny
to take pictures	сүрөткө тартуу	syrøtkø tartuu
to have one's picture taken	сүрөткө түшүү	syrøtkø tyʃyy

58. Shopping

to buy (purchase)	сатып алуу	satıp aluu
purchase	сатып алуу	satıp aluu
to go shopping	сатып алууга чыгуу	satıp aluuga ʧıguu
shopping	базарчылоо	bazarʧıloo

to be open (ab. store)	иштөө	iʃtøø
to be closed	жабылуу	dӡabıluu
footwear, shoes	бут кийим	but kijim
clothes, clothing	кийим-кече	kijim-keʧe

cosmetics	упа-эндик	upa-endik
food products	азык-түлүк	azık-tylyk
gift, present	белек	belek

| salesman | сатуучу | satuutʃu |
| saleswoman | сатуучу кыз | satuutʃu kız |

check out, cash desk	касса	kassa
mirror	күзгү	kyzgy
counter (store ~)	прилавок	prilavok
fitting room	кийим ченөөчү бөлмө	kijim tʃenøøtʃy bølmø

to try on	кийим ченөө	kijim tʃenøø
to fit (ab. dress, etc.)	ылайык келүү	ılajık kelyy
to like (I like …)	жактыруу	dʒaktıruu

price	баа	baa
price tag	баа	baa
to cost (vt)	туруу	turuu
How much?	Канча?	kantʃa?
discount	арзандатуу	arzandatuu

inexpensive (adj)	кымбат эмес	kımbat emes
cheap (adj)	арзан	arzan
expensive (adj)	кымбат	kımbat
It's expensive	Бул кымбат	bul kımbat

rental (n)	ижара	idʒara
to rent (~ a tuxedo)	ижарага алуу	idʒaraga aluu
credit (trade credit)	насыя	nasıja
on credit (adv)	насыяга алуу	nasıjaga aluu

59. Money

money	акча	aktʃa
currency exchange	алмаштыруу	almaʃtıruu
exchange rate	курс	kurs
ATM	банкомат	bankomat
coin	тыйын	tıjın

| dollar | доллар | dollar |
| euro | евро | evro |

lira	италиялык лира	italijalık lira
Deutschmark	немис маркасы	nemis markası
franc	франк	frank
pound sterling	фунт стерлинг	funt sterling
yen	йена	jena
debt	карыз	karız
debtor	карыздар	karızdar

| to lend (money) | карызга берүү | karızga beryy |
| to borrow (vi, vt) | карызга алуу | karızga aluu |

bank	банк	bank
account	эсеп	esep
to deposit (vt)	салуу	saluu
to deposit into the account	эсепке акча салуу	esepke aktʃa saluu
to withdraw (vt)	эсептен акча чыгаруу	esepten aktʃa tʃıgaruu

credit card	насыя картасы	nasıja kartası
cash	накталай акча	naktalaj aktʃa
check	чек	tʃek
to write a check	чек жазып берүү	tʃek dʒazıp beryy
checkbook	чек китепчеси	tʃek kiteptʃesi

wallet	намыян	namıjan
change purse	капчык	kaptʃık
safe	сейф	sejf

heir	мураскер	murasker
inheritance	мурас	muras
fortune (wealth)	мүлк	mylk

lease	ижара	idʒara
rent (money)	батир акысы	batir akısı
to rent (sth from sb)	батирге алуу	batirge aluu

price	баа	baa
cost	баа	baa
sum	сумма	summa

to spend (vt)	коротуу	korotuu
expenses	чыгым	tʃıgım
to economize (vi, vt)	үнөмдөө	ynømdøø
economical	сарамжал	saramdʒal

to pay (vi, vt)	төлөө	tøløø
payment	акы төлөө	akı tøløø
change (give the ~)	кайтарылган майда акча	kajtarılgan majda aktʃa

tax	салык	salık
fine	айып	ajıp
to fine (vt)	айып пул салуу	ajıp pul saluu

60. Post. Postal service

post office	почта	potʃta
mail (letters, etc.)	почта	potʃta
mailman	кат ташуучу	kat taʃuutʃu

opening hours	иш сааттары	iʃ saattarɪ
letter	кат	kat
registered letter	тапшырык кат	tapʃɪrɪk kat
postcard	открытка	otkrɪtka
telegram	телеграмма	telegramma
package (parcel)	посылка	posɪlka
money transfer	акча которуу	aktʃa kotoruu

to receive (vt)	алуу	aluu
to send (vt)	жөнөтүү	dʒønøtyy
sending	жөнөтүү	dʒønøtyy

address	дарек	darek
ZIP code	индекс	indeks
sender	жөнөтүүчү	dʒønøtyytʃy
receiver	алуучу	aluutʃu

| name (first name) | аты | atɪ |
| surname (last name) | фамилиясы | familijasɪ |

postage rate	тариф	tarif
standard (adj)	жөнөкөй	dʒønøkøj
economical (adj)	үнөмдүү	ynømdyy

weight	салмак	salmak
to weigh (~ letters)	таразалоо	tarazaloo
envelope	конверт	konvert
postage stamp	марка	marka
to stamp an envelope	марка жабыштыруу	marka dʒabɪʃtɪruu

Dwelling. House. Home

61. House. Electricity

electricity	электр кубаты	elektr kubatı
light bulb	чырак	ʧırak
switch	өчүргүч	øʧyrgyʧ
fuse (plug fuse)	эриме сактагыч	erime saktagıʧ
cable, wire (electric ~)	зым	zım
wiring	электр зымы	elektr zımı
electricity meter	электр эсептегич	elektr eseptegiʧ
readings	көрсөтүү ченем	kørsøtyy ʧenem

62. Villa. Mansion

country house	шаар четиндеги үй	ʃaar ʧetindegi yj
villa (seaside ~)	вилла	villa
wing (~ of a building)	канат	kanat
garden	бакча	bakʧa
park	сейил багы	sejil bagı
conservatory (greenhouse)	күнөскана	kynøskana
to look after (garden, etc.)	кароо	karoo
swimming pool	бассейн	bassejn
gym (home gym)	машыгуу залы	maʃıguu zalı
tennis court	теннис корту	tennis kortu
home theater (room)	кинотеатр	kinoteatr
garage	гараж	garadʒ
private property	жеке менчик	dʒeke menʧik
private land	жеке ээликте	dʒeke eelikte
warning (caution)	эскертүү	eskertyy
warning sign	эскертүү белгиси	eskertyy belgisi
security	күзөт	kyzøt
security guard	кароолчу	karoolʧu
burglar alarm	сигнализация	signalizaʦija

63. Apartment

apartment	батир	batir
room	бөлмө	bølmø
bedroom	уктоочу бөлмө	uktootʃu bølmø
dining room	ашкана	aʃkana
living room	конок үйү	konok yjy
study (home office)	иш бөлмөсү	iʃ bølmøsy
entry room	кире бериш	kire beriʃ
bathroom (room with a bath or shower)	ванная	vannaja
half bath	даараткана	daaratkana
ceiling	шып	ʃıp
floor	пол	pol
corner	бурч	burtʃ

64. Furniture. Interior

furniture	эмерек	emerek
table	стол	stol
chair	стул	stul
bed	керебет	kerebet
couch, sofa	диван	divan
armchair	олпок отургуч	olpok oturgutʃ
bookcase	китеп шкафы	kitep ʃkafı
shelf	текче	tektʃe
wardrobe	шкаф	ʃkaf
coat rack (wall-mounted ~)	кийим илгич	kijim ilgitʃ
coat stand	кийим илгич	kijim ilgitʃ
bureau, dresser	комод	komod
coffee table	журнал столу	dʒurnal stolu
mirror	күзгү	kyzgy
carpet	килем	kilem
rug, small carpet	килемче	kilemtʃe
fireplace	очок	otʃok
candle	шам	ʃam
candlestick	шамдал	ʃamdal
drapes	парда	parda
wallpaper	туш кагаз	tuʃ kagaz
blinds (jalousie)	жалюзи	dʒaldʒʉzi
table lamp	стол чырагы	stol tʃıragı

wall lamp (sconce)	чырак	tʃɪrak
floor lamp	торшер	torʃer
chandelier	асма шам	asma ʃam

leg (of chair, table)	бут	but
armrest	чыканак такооч	tʃɪkanak takootʃ
back (backrest)	жөлөнгүч	dʒøløngytʃ
drawer	суурма	suurma

65. Bedding

bedclothes	шейшеп	ʃejʃep
pillow	жаздык	dʒazdɪk
pillowcase	жаздык кап	dʒazdɪk kap
duvet, comforter	жууркан	dʒuurkan
sheet	шейшеп	ʃejʃep
bedspread	жапкыч	dʒapkɪtʃ

66. Kitchen

kitchen	ашкана	aʃkana
gas	газ	gaz
gas stove (range)	газ плитасы	gaz plitasɪ
electric stove	электр плитасы	elektr plitasɪ
oven	духовка	duxovka
microwave oven	микротолкун меши	mikrotolkun meʃi

refrigerator	муздаткыч	muzdatkɪtʃ
freezer	тоңдургуч	toŋdurgutʃ
dishwasher	идиш жуучу машина	idiʃ dʒuutʃu maʃina

meat grinder	эт туурагыч	et tuuragɪtʃ
juicer	шире сыккыч	ʃire sɪkkɪtʃ
toaster	тостер	toster
mixer	миксер	mikser

coffee machine	кофе кайнаткыч	kofe kajnatkɪtʃ
coffee pot	кофе кайнатуучу идиш	kofe kajnatuutʃu idiʃ
coffee grinder	кофе майдалагыч	kofe majdalagɪtʃ

kettle	чайнек	tʃajnek
teapot	чайнек	tʃajnek
lid	капкак	kapkak
tea strainer	чыпка	tʃɪpka

spoon	кашык	kaʃɪk
teaspoon	чай кашык	tʃaj kaʃɪk
soup spoon	аш кашык	aʃ kaʃɪk

| fork | вилка | vilka |
| knife | бычак | bɪtʃak |

tableware (dishes)	идиш-аяк	idiʃ-ajak
plate (dinner ~)	табак	tabak
saucer	табак	tabak

shot glass	рюмка	rʉmka
glass (tumbler)	ыстакан	ɪstakan
cup	чейчек	tʃøjtʃøk

sugar bowl	кум шекер салгыч	kum ʃeker salgɪtʃ
salt shaker	туз салгыч	tuz salgɪtʃ
pepper shaker	мурч салгыч	murtʃ salgɪtʃ
butter dish	май салгыч	maj salgɪtʃ

stock pot (soup pot)	мискей	miskej
frying pan (skillet)	табак	tabak
ladle	чемуч	tʃømytʃ
colander	депкир	depkir
tray (serving ~)	батыныс	batɪnɪs

bottle	бетелке	bøtølkø
jar (glass)	банка	banka
can	банка	banka

bottle opener	ачкыч	atʃkɪtʃ
can opener	ачкыч	atʃkɪtʃ
corkscrew	штопор	ʃtopor
filter	чыпка	tʃɪpka
to filter (vt)	чыпкалоо	tʃɪpkaloo

| trash, garbage (food waste, etc.) | таштанды | taʃtandɪ |
| trash can (kitchen ~) | таштанды чака | taʃtandɪ tʃaka |

67. Bathroom

bathroom	ванная	vannaja
water	суу	suu
faucet	чорго	tʃorgo
hot water	ысык суу	ɪsɪk suu
cold water	муздак суу	muzdak suu

toothpaste	тиш пастасы	tiʃ pastasɪ
to brush one's teeth	тиш жуу	tiʃ dʒuu
toothbrush	тиш щёткасы	tiʃ ʃtʃʲotkasɪ

| to shave (vi) | кырынуу | kɪrɪnuu |
| shaving foam | кырынуу үчүн көбүк | kɪrɪnuu ytʃyn købyk |

razor	устара	ustara
to wash (one's hands, etc.)	жуу	dʒuu
to take a bath	жуунуу	dʒuunuu
shower	душ	duʃ
to take a shower	душка түшүү	duʃka tyʃyy

bathtub	ванна	vanna
toilet (toilet bowl)	унитаз	unitaz
sink (washbasin)	раковина	rakovina

soap	самын	samın
soap dish	самын салгыч	samın salgıtʃ

sponge	губка	gubka
shampoo	шампунь	ʃampunʲ
towel	сүлгү	sylgy
bathrobe	халат	χalat

laundry (laundering)	кир жуу	kir dʒuu
washing machine	кир жуучу машина	kir dʒuutʃu maʃina
to do the laundry	кир жуу	kir dʒuu
laundry detergent	кир жуучу порошок	kir dʒuutʃu poroʃok

68. Household appliances

TV set	сыналгы	sınalgı
tape recorder	магнитофон	magnitofon
VCR (video recorder)	видеомагнитофон	videomagnitofon
radio	үналгы	ynalgı
player (CD, MP3, etc.)	плеер	pleer

video projector	видеопроектор	videoproektor
home movie theater	үй кинотеатры	yj kinoteatrı
DVD player	DVD ойноткуч	dividi ojnotkutʃ
amplifier	күчөткүч	kytʃøtkytʃ
video game console	оюн приставкасы	ojɯn pristavkası

video camera	видеокамера	videokamera
camera (photo)	фотоаппарат	fotoapparat
digital camera	санарип камерасы	sanarip kamerası

vacuum cleaner	чаң соргуч	tʃaŋ sorgutʃ
iron (e.g., steam ~)	үтүк	ytyk
ironing board	үтүктөөчү тактай	ytyktøøtʃy taktaj

telephone	телефон	telefon
cell phone	мобилдик	mobildik
typewriter	машинка	maʃinka
sewing machine	кийим тигүүчү машинка	kijim tigyytʃy maʃinka
microphone	микрофон	mikrofon

| headphones | кулакчын | kulaktʃın |
| remote control (TV) | пульт | pulʲt |

CD, compact disc	**CD, компакт-диск**	sidi, kompakt-disk
cassette, tape	**кассета**	kasseta
vinyl record	**пластинка**	plastinka

HUMAN ACTIVITIES

Job. Business. Part 1

69. Office. Working in the office

office (company ~)	офис	ofis
office (of director, etc.)	кабинет	kabinet
reception desk	кабыл алуу катчысы	kabıl aluu katʧısı
secretary	катчы	katʧı
secretary (fem.)	катчы аял	katʧı ajal
director	директор	direktor
manager	башкаруучу	baʃkaruutʃu
accountant	бухгалтер	buχgalter
employee	кызматкер	kızmatker
furniture	эмерек	emerek
desk	стол	stol
desk chair	кресло	kreslo
drawer unit	үкөк	ykøk
coat stand	кийим илгич	kijim ilgitʃ
computer	компьютер	kompjʉter
printer	принтер	printer
fax machine	факс	faks
photocopier	көчүрүүчү аппарат	køtʃyryytʃy apparat
paper	кагаз	kagaz
office supplies	кеңсе буюмдары	keŋse bujʉmdarı
mouse pad	килемче	kilemtʃe
sheet (of paper)	баракча	baraktʃa
binder	папка	papka
catalog	каталог	katalog
phone directory	абоненттердин тизмеси	abonentterdin tizmesi
documentation	документтер	dokumentter
brochure (e.g., 12 pages ~)	китепче	kiteptʃe
leaflet (promotional ~)	баракча	baraktʃa
sample	үлгү	ylgy
training meeting	окутуу	okutuu
meeting (of managers)	кеңеш	keŋeʃ
lunch time	түшкү танапис	tyʃky tanapis

to make a copy	кечүрмө алуу	køtʃyrmø aluu
to make multiple copies	көбөйтүү	købøjtyy
to receive a fax	факс алуу	faks aluu
to send a fax	факс жөнөтүү	faks dʒønøtyy

to call (by phone)	чалуу	tʃaluu
to answer (vt)	жооп берүү	dʒoop beryy
to put through	байланыштыруу	bajlanıʃtıruu

to arrange, to set up	уюштуруу	ujuʃturuu
to demonstrate (vt)	көрсөтүү	kørsøtyy
to be absent	келбей калуу	kelbej kaluu
absence	барбай калуу	barbaj kaluu

70. Business processes. Part 1

business	иш	iʃ
occupation	жумуш	dʒumuʃ

firm	фирма	firma
company	компания	kompanija
corporation	корпорация	korporatsija
enterprise	ишкана	iʃkana
agency	агенттик	agenttik

agreement (contract)	келишим	keliʃim
contract	контракт	kontrakt
deal	бүтүм	bytym
order (to place an ~)	буйрутма	bujrutma
terms (of the contract)	шарт	ʃart

wholesale (adv)	дүңү менен	dyŋy menen
wholesale (adj)	дүңүнөн	dyŋynøn
wholesale (n)	дүң соода	dyŋ sooda
retail (adj)	чекене	tʃekene
retail (n)	чекене соода	tʃekene sooda

competitor	атаандаш	ataandaʃ
competition	атаандаштык	ataandaʃtık
to compete (vi)	атаандашуу	ataandaʃuu

partner (associate)	өнөктөш	ønøktøʃ
partnership	өнөктөштүк	ønøktøʃtyk

crisis	каатчылык	kaattʃılık
bankruptcy	кудуретсиздик	kuduretsizdik
to go bankrupt	кудуретсиз калуу	kuduretsiz kaluu
difficulty	кыйынчылык	kıjıntʃılık
problem	көйгөй	køjgøj
catastrophe	киши көрбөсүн	kiʃi kørbøsyn

economy	экономика	ekonomika
economic (~ growth)	экономикалык	ekonomikalık
economic recession	экономикалык төмөндөө	ekonomikalık tømøndøø

| goal (aim) | максат | maksat |
| task | маселе | masele |

to trade (vi)	соодалашуу	soodalaʃuu
network (distribution ~)	тармак	tarmak
inventory (stock)	кампа	kampa
range (assortment)	ассортимент	assortiment

leader (leading company)	алдыӊкы катардагы	aldıŋkı katardagı
large (~ company)	ири	iri
monopoly	монополия	monopolija

theory	теория	teorija
practice	тажрыйба	tadʒrıjba
experience (in my ~)	тажрыйба	tadʒrıjba
trend (tendency)	умтулуу	umtuluu
development	өнүгүү	ønygyy

71. Business processes. Part 2

| profit (foregone ~) | пайда | pajda |
| profitable (~ deal) | майнаптуу | majnaptuu |

delegation (group)	делегация	delegatsija
salary	кызмат акы	kızmat akı
to correct (an error)	түзөтүү	tyzøtyy
business trip	иш сапар	iʃ sapar
commission	комиссия	komissija

to control (vt)	башкаруу	baʃkaruu
conference	иш жыйын	iʃ dʒıjın
license	лицензия	litsenzija
reliable (~ partner)	ишеничтүү	iʃenitʃtyy

initiative (undertaking)	демилге	demilge
norm (standard)	стандарт	standart
circumstance	жагдай	dʒagdaj
duty (of employee)	милдет	mildet

organization (company)	уюм	ujʉm
organization (process)	уюштуруу	ujʉʃturuu
organized (adj)	уюштурулган	ujʉʃturulgan
cancellation	токтотуу	toktotuu
to cancel (call off)	жокко чыгаруу	dʒokko tʃıgaruu
report (official ~)	отчет	ottʃet

patent	патент	patent
to patent (obtain patent)	патентөө	patentøø
to plan (vt)	пландаштыруу	plandaʃtıruu

bonus (money)	сыйлык	sıjlık
professional (adj)	кесипкөй	kesipkøj
procedure	тартип	tartip

to examine (contract, etc.)	карап чыгуу	karap ʧıguu
calculation	эсеп-кысап	esep-kısap
reputation	аброй	abroj
risk	тобокел	tobokel

to manage, to run	башкаруу	baʃkaruu
information (report)	маалымат	maalımat
property	менчик	menʧik
union	бирикме	birikme

life insurance	жашоону камсыздандыруу	dʒaʃoonu kamsızdandıruu
to insure (vt)	камсыздандыруу	kamsızdandıruu
insurance	камсыздандыруу	kamsızdandıruu

auction (~ sale)	тоорук	tooruk
to notify (inform)	билдирүү	bildiryy
management (process)	башкаруу	baʃkaruu
service (~ industry)	кызмат	kızmat

forum	форум	forum
to function (vi)	иш-милдетти аткаруу	iʃ-mildetti atkaruu
stage (phase)	кадам	kadam
legal (~ services)	укуктуу	ukuktuu
lawyer (legal advisor)	юрист	jʉrist

72. Production. Works

plant	завод	zavod
factory	фабрика	fabrika
workshop	цех	tseχ
works, production site	өндүрүш	øndyryʃ

industry (manufacturing)	өнөр-жай	ønør-dʒaj
industrial (adj)	өнөр-жай	ønør-dʒaj
heavy industry	оор өнөр-жай	oor ønør-dʒaj
light industry	жеңил өнөр-жай	dʒeŋil ønør-dʒaj

products	өндүрүм	øndyrym
to produce (vt)	өндүрүү	øndyryy
raw materials	чийки зат	ʧijki zat
foreman (construction ~)	бригадир	brigadir

| workers team (crew) | бригада | brigada |
| worker | жумушчу | dʒumuʃtʃu |

working day	иш күнү	iʃ kyny
pause (rest break)	тыныгуу	tınıguu
meeting	чогулуш	tʃoguluʃ
to discuss (vt)	талкуулоо	talkuuloo

plan	план	plan
to fulfill the plan	планды аткаруу	plandı atkaruu
rate of output	иштеп чыгаруу коюму	iʃtep tʃigaruu kojɵmu
quality	сапат	sapat
control (checking)	текшерүү	tekʃeryy
quality control	сапат текшерүү	sapat tekʃeryy

workplace safety	эмгек коопсуздугу	emgek koopsuzdugu
discipline	тартип	tartip
violation	бузуу	buzuu
(of safety rules, etc.)		

to violate (rules)	бузуу	buzuu
strike	ишти калтыруу	iʃti kaltıruu
striker	иш калтыргыч	iʃ kaltırgıtʃ
to be on strike	ишти калтыруу	iʃti kaltıruu
labor union	профсоюз	profsojɵz

to invent (machine, etc.)	ойлоп табуу	ojlop tabuu
invention	ойлоп табылган нерсе	ojlop tabılgan nerse
research	изилдөө	izildøø
to improve (make better)	жакшыртуу	dʒakʃırtuu
technology	технология	teχnologija
technical drawing	чийме	tʃijme

load, cargo	жүк	dʒyk
loader (person)	жүк ташуучу	dʒyk taʃuutʃu
to load (vehicle, etc.)	жүктөө	dʒyktøø
loading (process)	жүктөө	dʒyktøø
to unload (vi, vt)	жүк түшүрүү	dʒyk tyʃuryy
unloading	жүк түшүрүү	dʒyk tyʃyryy

transportation	транспорт	transport
transportation company	транспорттук компания	transporttuk kompanija
to transport (vt)	транспорт менен ташуу	transport menen taʃuu

freight car	вагон	vagon
tank (e.g., oil ~)	цистерна	tsısterna
truck	жүк ташуучу машина	dʒyk taʃuutʃu maʃina

machine tool	станок	stanok
mechanism	механизм	meχanizm
industrial waste	таштандылар	taʃtandılar
packing (process)	таңгактоо	taŋgaktoo
to pack (vt)	таңгактоо	taŋgaktoo

73. Contract. Agreement

contract	контракт	kontrakt
agreement	макулдашуу	makuldaʃuu
addendum	тиркеме	tirkeme
to sign a contract	контракт түзүү	kontrakt tyzyy
signature	кол тамга	kol tamga
to sign (vt)	кол коюу	kol kojʉu
seal (stamp)	мөөр	møør
subject of the contract	келишимдин предмети	keliʃimdin predmeti
clause	пункт	punkt
parties (in contract)	тараптар	taraptar
legal address	юридикалык дарек	jʉridikalık darek
to violate the contract	контрактты бузуу	kontrakttı buzuu
commitment (obligation)	милдеттенме	mildettenme
responsibility	жоопкерчилик	dʒoopkertʃilik
force majeure	форс-мажор	fors-madʒor
dispute	талаш	talaʃ
penalties	жаза чаралары	dʒaza tʃaraları

74. Import & Export

import	импорт	import
importer	импорттоочу	importtootʃu
to import (vt)	импорттоо	importtoo
import (as adj.)	импорт	import
export (exportation)	экспорт	eksport
exporter	экспорттоочу	eksporttootʃu
to export (vi, vt)	экспорттоо	eksporttoo
export (as adj.)	экспорт	eksport
goods (merchandise)	товар	tovar
consignment, lot	жүк тобу	dʒyk tobu
weight	салмак	salmak
volume	көлөм	køløm
cubic meter	куб метр	kub metr
manufacturer	өндүрүүчү	øndyryytʃy
transportation company	транспорттук компания	transporttuk kompanija
container	контейнер	kontejner
border	чек ара	tʃek ara
customs	бажыкана	badʒıkana
customs duty	бажы салык	badʒı salık

customs officer	бажы кызматкери	badʒı kızmatkeri
smuggling	контрабанда	kontrabanda
contraband	контрабанда	kontrabanda
(smuggled goods)		

75. Finances

stock (share)	акция	aktsija
bond (certificate)	баалуу кагаздар	baaluu kagazdar
promissory note	вексель	vekselʲ

| stock exchange | биржа | birdʒa |
| stock price | акциялар курсу | aktsijalar kursu |

to go down	арзандоо	arzandoo
(become cheaper)		
to go up (become	кымбаттоо	kımbattoo
more expensive)		

| share | үлүш | ylyʃ |
| controlling interest | башкаруучу пакет | baʃkaruutʃu paket |

investment	салым	salım
to invest (v)	салым кылуу	salım kıluu
percent	пайыз	pajız
interest (on investment)	пайыз менен пайда	pajız menen pajda

profit	пайда	pajda
profitable (adj)	майнаптуу	majnaptuu
tax	салык	salık

currency (foreign ~)	валюта	valʉta
national (adj)	улуттук	uluttuk
exchange (currency ~)	алмаштыруу	almaʃtıruu

| accountant | бухгалтер | buχgalter |
| accounting | бухгалтерия | buχgalterija |

bankruptcy	кудуретсиздик	kuduretsizdik
collapse, crash	кыйроо	kıjroo
ruin	жакырдануу	dʒakırdanuu
to be ruined (financially)	жакырдануу	dʒakırdanuu
inflation	инфляция	inflʲatsija
devaluation	девальвация	devalʲvatsija

capital	капитал	kapital
income	киреше	kireʃe
turnover	жүгүртүлүш	dʒygyrtylyʃ
resources	такоолдор	takooldor
monetary resources	акча каражаттары	aktʃa karadʒattarı

| overhead | кошумча чыгашалар | koʃumtʃa tʃɨgaʃalar |
| to reduce (expenses) | кыскартуу | kɨskartuu |

76. Marketing

marketing	базар таануу	bazar taanuu
market	базар	bazar
market segment	базар сегменти	bazar segmenti
product	өнүм	ønym
goods (merchandise)	товар	tovar
brand	соода маркасы	sooda markasɨ
trademark	соода маркасы	sooda markasɨ
logotype	фирмалык белги	firmalɨk belgi
logo	логотип	logotip
demand	талап	talap
supply	сунуш	sunuʃ
need	керек	kerek
consumer	керектөөчү	kerektøøtʃy
analysis	талдоо	taldoo
to analyze (vt)	талдоо	taldoo
positioning	турак табуу	turak tabuu
to position (vt)	турак табуу	turak tabuu
price	баа	baa
pricing policy	баа саясаты	baa sajasatɨ
price formation	баа чыгаруу	baa tʃɨgaruu

77. Advertising

advertising	жарнама	dʒarnama
to advertise (vt)	жарнамалоо	dʒarnamaloo
budget	бюджет	bʉdʒet
ad, advertisement	жарнама	dʒarnama
TV advertising	теле жарнама	tele dʒarnama
radio advertising	радио жарнама	radio dʒarnama
outdoor advertising	сырткы жарнама	sɨrtkɨ dʒarnama
mass media	масс медиа	mass medija
periodical (n)	мезгилдүү басылма	mezgildyy basɨlma
image (public appearance)	имидж	imidʒ
slogan	лозунг	lozung
motto (maxim)	ураан	uraan
campaign	кампания	kampanija

advertising campaign	жарнамалык кампания	dʒarnamalık kampanija
target group	максаттуу топ	maksattuu top

business card	тааныТма	taanıtma
leaflet (promotional ~)	баракча	baraktʃa
brochure (e.g., 12 pages ~)	китепче	kiteptʃe
pamphlet	кат-кат китепче	kat-kat kiteptʃe
newsletter	бюллетень	bᵾlletenʲ

signboard (store sign, etc.)	көрнөк	kørnøk
poster	көрнөк	kørnøk
billboard	жарнамалык такта	dʒarnamalık takta

78. Banking

bank	банк	bank
branch (of bank, etc.)	бөлүм	bølym

bank clerk, consultant	кеңешчи	keŋeʃtʃi
manager (director)	башкаруучу	baʃkaruutʃu

bank account	эсеп	esep
account number	эсеп номери	esep nomeri
checking account	учурдагы эсеп	utʃurdagı esep
savings account	топтолмо эсеп	toptolmo esep

to open an account	эсеп ачуу	esep atʃuu
to close the account	эсеп жабуу	esep dʒabuu
to deposit into the account	эсепке акча салуу	esepke aktʃa saluu
to withdraw (vt)	эсептен акча чыгаруу	esepten aktʃa tʃıgaruu

deposit	аманат	amanat
to make a deposit	аманат кылуу	amanat kıluu
wire transfer	акча которуу	aktʃa kotoruu
to wire, to transfer	акча которуу	aktʃa kotoruu

sum	сумма	summa
How much?	Канча?	kantʃa?

signature	кол тамга	kol tamga
to sign (vt)	кол коюу	kol kojᵾu

credit card	насыя картасы	nasıja kartası
code (PIN code)	код	kod
credit card number	насыя картанын номери	nasıja kartanın nomeri

ATM	банкомат	bankomat
check	чек	tʃek
to write a check	чек жазып берүү	tʃek dʒazıp beryy

checkbook	чек китепчеси	ʧek kitepʧesi
loan (bank ~)	насыя	nasija
to apply for a loan	насыя үчүн кайрылуу	nasija yʧyn kajrıluu
to get a loan	насыя алуу	nasija aluu
to give a loan	насыя берүү	nasija beryy
guarantee	кепилдик	kepildik

79. Telephone. Phone conversation

telephone	телефон	telefon
cell phone	мобилдик	mobildik
answering machine	автоматтык жооп берүүчү	avtomattık dʒoop beryyʧy
to call (by phone)	чалуу	ʧaluu
phone call	чакыруу	ʧakıruu
to dial a number	номер терүү	nomer teryy
Hello!	Алло!	allo!
to ask (vt)	суроо	suroo
to answer (vi, vt)	жооп берүү	dʒoop beryy
to hear (vt)	угуу	uguu
well (adv)	жакшы	dʒakʃı
not well (adv)	жаман	dʒaman
noises (interference)	ызы-чуу	ızı-ʧuu
receiver	трубка	trubka
to pick up (~ the phone)	трубканы алуу	trubkanı aluu
to hang up (~ the phone)	трубканы коюу	trubkanı kojuu
busy (engaged)	бош эмес	boʃ emes
to ring (ab. phone)	шыңгыроо	ʃıŋgıroo
telephone book	телефондук китепче	telefonduk kiteptʃe
local (adj)	жергиликтүү	dʒergiliktyy
local call	жергиликтүү чакыруу	dʒergiliktyy ʧakıruu
long distance (~ call)	шаар аралык	ʃaar aralık
long-distance call	шаар аралык чакыруу	ʃaar aralık ʧakıruu
international (adj)	эл аралык	el aralık
international call	эл аралык чакыруу	el aralık ʧakıruu

80. Cell phone

cell phone	мобилдик	mobildik
display	дисплей	displej
button	баскыч	baskıʧ
SIM card	SIM-карта	sim-karta

battery	батарея	batareja
to be dead (battery)	зарядканын түгөнүүсү	zarʲadkanın tygønyysy
charger	заряддоочу шайман	zarʲaddooʧu ʃajman

menu	меню	menʉ
settings	орнотуулар	ornotuular
tune (melody)	обон	obon
to select (м)	тандоо	tandoo

calculator	калькулятор	kalʲkulʲator
voice mail	автоматтык жооп бергич	avtomattık dʒoop bergiʧ
alarm clock	ойготкуч	ojgotkuʧ
contacts	байланыштар	bajlanıʃtar

SMS (text message)	SMS-кабар	esemes-kabar
subscriber	абонент	abonent

81. Stationery

ballpoint pen	калем сап	kalem sap
fountain pen	калем уч	kalem uʧ

pencil	карандаш	karandaʃ
highlighter	маркер	marker
felt-tip pen	фломастер	flomaster

notepad	дептерче	depterʧe
agenda (diary)	күндөлүк	kyndølyk

ruler	сызгыч	sızgıʧ
calculator	калькулятор	kalʲkulʲator
eraser	өчүргүч	øʧyrgyʧ
thumbtack	кнопка	knopka
paper clip	кыскыч	kıskıʧ

glue	желим	dʒelim
stapler	степлер	stepler
hole punch	тешкич	teʃkiʧ
pencil sharpener	учтагыч	uʧtagıʧ

82. Kinds of business

accounting services	бухгалтердик кызмат	buχgalterdik kızmat
advertising	жарнама	dʒarnama
advertising agency	жарнама агенттиги	dʒarnama agenttigi
air-conditioners	аба желдеткичтер	aba dʒeldetkiʧter
airline	авиакомпания	aviakompanija

alcoholic beverages	алкоголь ичимдиктери	alkogolʲ itʃimdikteri
antiques (antique dealers)	антиквариат	antikvariat
art gallery (contemporary ~)	арт-галерея	art-galereja
audit services	аудиторлук кызмат	auditorluk kızmat
banking industry	банк бизнеси	bank biznesi
bar	бар	bar
beauty parlor	сулуулук салону	suluuluk salonu
bookstore	китеп дүкөнү	kitep dykøny
brewery	сыра чыгаруучу жай	sıra tʃɪgaruutʃu ʤaj
business center	бизнес-борбор	biznes-borbor
business school	бизнес-мектеп	biznes-mektep
casino	казино	kazino
construction	курулуш	kuruluʃ
consulting	консалтинг	konsalting
dental clinic	стоматология	stomatologija
design	дизайн	dizajn
drugstore, pharmacy	дарыкана	darıkana
dry cleaners	химиялык тазалоо	χimijalık tazaloo
employment agency	кадрдык агенттиги	kadrdık agenttigi
financial services	каржылык кызматтар	karʤılık kızmattar
food products	азык-түлүк	azık-tylyk
funeral home	ырасым бюросу	ırasım bʉrosu
furniture (e.g., house ~)	эмерек	emerek
clothing, garment	кийим	kijim
hotel	мейманкана	mejmankana
ice-cream	бал муздак	bal muzdak
industry (manufacturing)	өнөр-жай	ønør-ʤaj
insurance	камсыздандыруу	kamsızdandıruu
Internet	интернет	internet
investments (finance)	салымдар	salımdar
jeweler	зергер	zerger
jewelry	зер буюмдар	zer bujʉmdar
laundry (shop)	кир жуу ишканасы	kir ʤuu iʃkanası
legal advisor	юридикалык кызматтар	jʉridikalık kızmattar
light industry	жеңил өнөр-жай	ʤeŋil ønør-ʤaj
magazine	журнал	ʤurnal
mail order selling	каталог боюнча соода-сатык	katalog bojʉntʃa sooda-satık
medicine	медицина	meditsina
movie theater	кинотеатр	kinoteatr
museum	музей	muzej
news agency	жаңылыктар агенттиги	ʤaŋılıktar agenttigi
newspaper	гезит	gezit

nightclub	түнкү клуб	tyŋky klub
oil (petroleum)	мунайзат	munajzat
courier services	чабармандык кызматы	ʧabarmandık kızmatı
pharmaceutics	фармацевтика	farmaʦevtika
printing (industry)	полиграфия	poligrafija
publishing house	басмакана	basmakana
radio (~ station)	үналгы	ynalgı
real estate	кыймылсыз мүлк	kıjmılsız mylk
restaurant	ресторан	restoran
security company	күзөт агенттиги	kyzøt agenttigi
sports	спорт	sport
stock exchange	биржа	birdʒa
store	дүкөн	dykøn
supermarket	супермаркет	supermarket
swimming pool (public ~)	бассейн	bassejn
tailor shop	ателье	atelje
television	телекөрсөтүү	telekørsøtyy
theater	театр	teatr
trade (commerce)	соода	sooda
transportation	ташып жеткирүү	taʃıp dʒetkiryy
travel	туризм	turizm
veterinarian	мал доктуру	mal dokturu
warehouse	кампа	kampa
waste collection	таштанды чыгаруу	taʃtandı ʧıgaruu

Job. Business. Part 2

83. Show. Exhibition

exhibition, show	көргөзмө	kørgøzmø
trade show	соода көргөзмөсү	sooda kørgøzmøsy
participation	катышуу	katıʃuu
to participate (vi)	катышуу	katıʃuu
participant (exhibitor)	катышуучу	katıʃuutʃu
director	директор	direktor
organizers' office	уюштуруу комитети	ujuʃturuu komiteti
organizer	уюштуруучу	ujuʃturuutʃu
to organize (vt)	уюштуруу	ujuʃturuu
participation form	катышууга ынта билдирмеси	katıʃuuga ınta bildirmesi
to fill out (vt)	толтуруу	tolturuu
details	ийне-жиби	ijne-dʒibi
information	маалымат	maalımat
price (cost, rate)	баа	baa
including	кошуп	koʃup
to include (vt)	кошулган	koʃulgan
to pay (vi, vt)	төлөө	tøløø
registration fee	каттоо төгүмү	kattoo tøgymy
entrance	кирүү	kiryy
pavilion, hall	павильон	pavilʲon
to register (vt)	каттоо	kattoo
badge (identity tag)	төшбелги	tøʃbelgi
booth, stand	көргөзмө стенди	kørgøzmø stendi
to reserve, to book	камдык буйрутмалоо	kamdık bujrutmaloo
display case	айнек стенд	ajnek stend
spotlight	чырак	tʃırak
design	дизайн	dizajn
to place (put, set)	жайгаштыруу	dʒajgaʃtıruu
to be placed	жайгашуу	dʒajgaʃuu
distributor	дистрибьютор	distribjutor
supplier	жеткирип берүүчү	dʒetkirip beryytʃy
to supply (vt)	жеткирип берүү	dʒetkirip beryy
country	өлкө	ølkø

| foreign (adj) | чет өлкөлүк | tʃet ølkølyk |
| product | өнүм | ønym |

association	ассоциация	assotsiatsija
conference hall	конференц-зал	konferents-zal
congress	конгресс	kongress
contest (competition)	жарыш	dʒarıʃ

visitor (attendee)	келүүчү	kelyytʃy
to visit (attend)	баш багуу	baʃ baguu
customer	кардар	kardar

84. Science. Research. Scientists

science	илим	ilim
scientific (adj)	илимий	ilimij
scientist	илимпоз	ilimpoz
theory	теория	teorija

axiom	аксиома	aksioma
analysis	талдоо	taldoo
to analyze (vt)	талдоо	taldoo
argument (strong ~)	далил	dalil
substance (matter)	зат	zat

hypothesis	гипотеза	gipoteza
dilemma	дилемма	dilemma
dissertation	диссертация	dissertatsija
dogma	догма	dogma

doctrine	доктрина	doktrina
research	изилдөө	izildøø
to research (vt)	изилдөө	izildøø
tests (laboratory ~)	сынак	sınak
laboratory	лаборатория	laboratorija

method	ыкма	ıkma
molecule	молекула	molekula
monitoring	бейлөө	bejløø
discovery (act, event)	таап ачуу	taap atʃuu

postulate	постулат	postulat
principle	усул	usul
forecast	божомол	bodʒomol
to forecast (vt)	алдын ала айтуу	aldın ala ajtuu

synthesis	синтез	sintez
trend (tendency)	умтулуу	umtuluu
theorem	теорема	teorema
teachings	окуу	okuu

fact	**далил**	dalil
expedition	**экспедиция**	ekspeditsija
experiment	**тажрыйба**	tadʒrıjba
academician	**академик**	akademik
bachelor (e.g., ~ of Arts)	**бакалавр**	bakalavr
doctor (PhD)	**доктор**	doktor
Associate Professor	**доцент**	dotsent
Master (e.g., ~ of Arts)	**магистр**	magistr
professor	**профессор**	professor

Professions and occupations

85. Job search. Dismissal

job	иш	iʃ
staff (work force)	жамаат	dʒamaat
personnel	жамаат курамы	dʒamaat kuramı
career	мансап	mansap
prospects (chances)	перспектива	perspektiva
skills (mastery)	чеберчилик	tʃebertʃilik
selection (screening)	тандоо	tandoo
employment agency	кадрдык агенттиги	kadrdık agenttigi
résumé	таржымал	tardʒımal
job interview	аңгемелешүү	aŋgemeleʃyy
vacancy, opening	жумуш орун	dʒumuʃ orun
salary, pay	эмгек акы	emgek akı
fixed salary	маяна	majana
pay, compensation	акысын төлөө	akısın tøløø
position (job)	кызмат орун	kızmat orun
duty (of employee)	милдет	mildet
range of duties	милдеттенмелер	mildettenmeler
busy (I'm ~)	бош эмес	boʃ emes
to fire (dismiss)	бошотуу	boʃotuu
dismissal	бошотуу	boʃotuu
unemployment	жумушсуздук	dʒumuʃsuzduk
unemployed (n)	жумушсуз	dʒumuʃsuz
retirement	баяракы	baarakı
to retire (from job)	ардактуу эс алууга чыгуу	ardaktuu es aluuga tʃıguu

86. Business people

director	директор	direktor
manager (director)	башкаруучу	baʃkaruutʃu
boss	башкаруучу	baʃkaruutʃu
superior	башчы	baʃtʃı
superiors	башчылар	baʃtʃılar

| president | президент | prezident |
| chairman | төрага | tøraga |

deputy (substitute)	орун басар	orun basar
assistant	жардамчы	dʒardamtʃɪ
secretary	катчы	kattʃɪ
personal assistant	жеке катчы	dʒeke kattʃɪ

businessman	бизнесмен	biznesmen
entrepreneur	ишкер	iʃker
founder	негиздөөчү	negizdøøtʃy
to found (vt)	негиздөө	negizdøø

incorporator	уюмдаштыруучу	ujʉmdaʃtɪruutʃu
partner	өнөктөш	ønøktøʃ
stockholder	акция кармоочу	aktsija karmootʃu

millionaire	миллионер	millioner
billionaire	миллиардер	milliarder
owner, proprietor	ээси	eesi
landowner	жер ээси	dʒer eesi

client	кардар	kardar
regular client	туруктуу кардар	turuktuu kardar
buyer (customer)	сатып алуучу	satɪp aluutʃu
visitor	келүүчү	kelyytʃy

professional (n)	кесипкөй	kesipkøj
expert	ишбилги	iʃbilgi
specialist	адис	adis

| banker | банкир | bankir |
| broker | далдалчы | daldaltʃɪ |

cashier, teller	кассир	kassir
accountant	бухгалтер	buxgalter
security guard	кароолчу	karooltʃu

investor	салым кошуучу	salɪm koʃuutʃu
debtor	карыздар	karɪzdar
creditor	насыя алуучу	nasɪja aluutʃu
borrower	карызга алуучу	karɪzga aluutʃu

| importer | импорттоочу | importtootʃu |
| exporter | экспорттоочу | eksporttootʃu |

manufacturer	өндүрүүчү	øndyryytʃy
distributor	дистрибьютор	distribjʉtor
middleman	ортомчу	ortomtʃu

| consultant | кеңешчи | keŋeʃtʃi |
| sales representative | сатуу агенти | satuu agenti |

| agent | агент | agent |
| insurance agent | камсыздандыруучу агент | kamsızdandıruutʃu agent |

87. Service professions

cook	ашпозчу	aʃpoztʃu
chef (kitchen chef)	башкы ашпозчу	baʃkı aʃpoztʃu
baker	навайчы	navajtʃı

bartender	бармен	barmen
waiter	официант	ofitsiant
waitress	официант кыз	ofitsiant kız

lawyer, attorney	жактоочу	dʒaktootʃu
lawyer (legal expert)	юрист	jurist
notary public	нотариус	notarius

electrician	электрик	elektrik
plumber	сантехник	santeχnik
carpenter	жыгач уста	dʒıgatʃ usta

masseur	укалоочу	ukalootʃu
masseuse	укалоочу	ukalootʃu
doctor	доктур	doktur

taxi driver	такси айдоочу	taksi ajdootʃu
driver	айдоочу	ajdootʃu
delivery man	жеткирүүчү	dʒetkiryytʃy

chambermaid	үй кызматкери	yj kızmatkeri
security guard	кароолчу	karooltʃu
flight attendant (fem.)	стюардесса	stuardessa

schoolteacher	мугалим	mugalim
librarian	китепканачы	kitepkanatʃı
translator	котормочу	kotormotʃu

| interpreter | оозеки котормочу | oozeki kotormotʃu |
| guide | гид | gid |

hairdresser	чач тарач	tʃatʃ taratʃ
mailman	кат ташуучу	kat taʃuutʃu
salesman (store staff)	сатуучу	satuutʃu

| gardener | багбанчы | bagbantʃı |
| domestic servant | үй кызматчы | yj kızmattʃı |

| maid (female servant) | үй кызматчы аял | yj kızmattʃı ajal |
| cleaner (cleaning lady) | тазалагыч | tazalagıtʃ |

88. Military professions and ranks

private	катардагы жоокер	katardagı dʒooker
sergeant	сержант	serdʒant
lieutenant	лейтенант	lejtenant
captain	капитан	kapitan

major	майор	major
colonel	полковник	polkovnik
general	генерал	general
marshal	маршал	marʃal
admiral	адмирал	admiral

military (n)	аскер кызматчысы	asker kızmatʧısı
soldier	аскер	asker
officer	офицер	ofitser
commander	командир	komandir

border guard	чек арачы	ʧek araʧı
radio operator	радист	radist
scout (searcher)	чалгынчы	ʧalgınʧı
pioneer (sapper)	сапёр	sapʲor
marksman	аткыч	atkıʧ
navigator	штурман	ʃturman

89. Officials. Priests

| king | король, падыша | korolʲ, padıʃa |
| queen | ханыша | χanıʃa |

| prince | канзаада | kanzaada |
| princess | ханбийке | χanbijke |

| czar | падыша | padıʃa |
| czarina | ханыша | χanıʃa |

president	президент	prezident
Secretary (minister)	министр	ministr
prime minister	премьер-министр	premjer-ministr
senator	сенатор	senator

diplomat	дипломат	diplomat
consul	консул	konsul
ambassador	элчи	elʧi

| counselor (diplomatic officer) | кеңешчи | keŋeʃʧi |
| official, functionary (civil servant) | аткаминер | atkaminer |

prefect	префект	prefekt
mayor	мэр	mer

judge	сот	sot
prosecutor (e.g., district attorney)	прокурор	prokuror

missionary	миссионер	missioner
monk	кечил	ketʃil
abbot	аббат	abbat
rabbi	раввин	ravvin

vizier	визирь	viziri
shah	шах	ʃaχ
sheikh	шейх	ʃejχ

90. Agricultural professions

beekeeper	балчы	balʧı
herder, shepherd	чабан	ʧaban
agronomist	агроном	agronom
cattle breeder	малчы	malʧı
veterinarian	мал доктуру	mal dokturu

farmer	фермер	fermer
winemaker	вино жасоочу	vino dʒasooʧu
zoologist	зоолог	zoolog
cowboy	ковбой	kovboj

91. Art professions

actor	актёр	aktior
actress	актриса	aktrisa

singer (masc.)	ырчы	ırʧı
singer (fem.)	ырчы кыз	ırʧı kız

dancer (masc.)	бийчи жигит	bijʧi dʒigit
dancer (fem.)	бийчи кыз	bijʧi kız

performer (masc.)	аткаруучу	atkaruutʃu
performer (fem.)	аткаруучу	atkaruutʃu

musician	музыкант	muzıkant
pianist	пианист	pianist
guitar player	гитарист	gitarist
conductor (orchestra ~)	дирижёр	diridʒior
composer	композитор	kompozitor

impresario	импресарио	impresario
film director	режиссёр	redʒissʲor
producer	продюсер	produser
scriptwriter	сценарист	stsenarist
critic	сынчы	sɪntʃɪ

writer	жазуучу	dʒazuutʃu
poet	акын	akɪn
sculptor	бедизчи	bedizʧi
artist (painter)	сүрөтчү	syrøttʃy

juggler	жонглёр	dʒonglʲor
clown	маскарапоз	maskarapoz
acrobat	акробат	akrobat
magician	көз боечу	køz boetʃu

92. Various professions

doctor	доктур	doktur
nurse	медсестра	medsestra
psychiatrist	психиатр	psiχiatr
dentist	тиш доктур	tiʃ doktur
surgeon	хирург	χirurg

astronaut	астронавт	astronavt
astronomer	астроном	astronom
pilot	учкуч	utʃkutʃ

driver (of taxi, etc.)	айдоочу	ajdootʃu
engineer (train driver)	машинист	maʃinist
mechanic	механик	meχanik

miner	кенчи	kentʃi
worker	жумушчу	dʒumuʃtʃu
locksmith	слесарь	slesarʲ
joiner (carpenter)	жыгач уста	dʒɪgatʃ usta
turner (lathe operator)	токарь	tokarʲ
construction worker	куруучу	kuruutʃu
welder	ширеткич	ʃiretkitʃ

professor (title)	профессор	professor
architect	архитектор	arχitektor
historian	тарыхчы	tarɪχtʃɪ
scientist	илимпоз	ilimpoz
physicist	физик	fizik
chemist (scientist)	химик	χimik

archeologist	археолог	arχeolog
geologist	геолог	geolog
researcher (scientist)	изилдөөчү	izildøøtʃy

| babysitter | бала баккыч | bala bakkıtʃ |
| teacher, educator | мугалим | mugalim |

editor	редактор	redaktor
editor-in-chief	башкы редактор	baʃkı redaktor
correspondent	кабарчы	kabartʃı
typist (fem.)	машинистка	maʃinistka

designer	дизайнер	dizajner
computer expert	компьютер адиси	kompjʉter adisi
programmer	программист	programmist
engineer (designer)	инженер	indʒener

sailor	деңизчи	deŋiztʃi
seaman	матрос	matros
rescuer	куткаруучу	kutkaruutʃu

fireman	өрт өчүргүч	ørt øtʃyrgytʃ
police officer	полиция кызматкери	politsija kızmatkeri
watchman	кароолчу	karooltʃu
detective	аңдуучу	aŋduutʃu

customs officer	бажы кызматкери	badʒı kızmatkeri
bodyguard	жан сакчы	dʒan saktʃı
prison guard	кузөтчу	kyzøttʃy
inspector	инспектор	inspektor

sportsman	спортчу	sporttʃu
trainer, coach	машыктыруучу	maʃıktıruutʃu
butcher	касапчы	kasaptʃı
cobbler (shoe repairer)	өтүкчү	øtyktʃy
merchant	жеке соодагер	dʒeke soodager
loader (person)	жүк ташуучу	dʒyk taʃuutʃu

| fashion designer | модельер | modeljer |
| model (fem.) | модель | modelʲ |

93. Occupations. Social status

| schoolboy | окуучу | okuutʃu |
| student (college ~) | студент | student |

philosopher	философ	filosof
economist	экономист	ekonomist
inventor	ойлоп табуучу	ojlop tabuutʃu

unemployed (n)	жумушсуз	dʒumuʃsuz
retiree	бааргер	baarger
spy, secret agent	тыңчы	tıŋtʃı
prisoner	камактагы адам	kamaktagı adam

striker	иш калтыргыч	iʃ kaltırgıtʃ
bureaucrat	бюрократ	bʉrokrat
traveler (globetrotter)	саякатчы	sajakattʃı

gay, homosexual (n)	гомосексуалист	gomoseksualist
hacker	хакер	χaker
hippie	хиппи	χippi

bandit	ууру-кески	uuru-keski
hit man, killer	жалданма киши өлтүргүч	dʒaldanma kiʃi øltyrgytʃ
drug addict	баңги	baŋgi
drug dealer	баңгизат сатуучу	baŋgizat satuutʃu
prostitute (fem.)	сойку	sojku
pimp	жан бакты	dʒan baktı

sorcerer	жадыгөй	dʒadıgøj
sorceress (evil ~)	жадыгөй	dʒadıgøj
pirate	деңиз каракчысы	deŋiz karaktʃısı
slave	кул	kul
samurai	самурай	samuraj
savage (primitive)	жапайы	dʒapajı

Education

94. School

school	мектеп	mektep
principal (headmaster)	мектеп директору	mektep direktoru
pupil (boy)	окуучу бала	okuuʧu bala
pupil (girl)	окуучу кыз	okuuʧu kız
schoolboy	окуучу	okuuʧu
schoolgirl	окуучу кыз	okuuʧu kız
to teach (sb)	окутуу	okutuu
to learn (language, etc.)	окуу	okuu
to learn by heart	жаттоо	dʒattoo
to learn (~ to count, etc.)	үйрөнүү	yjrønyy
to be in school	мектепке баруу	mektepke baruu
to go to school	окууга баруу	okuuga baruu
alphabet	алфавит	alfavit
subject (at school)	сабак	sabak
classroom	класс	klass
lesson	сабак	sabak
recess	танапис	tanapis
school bell	коңгуроо	koŋguroo
school desk	парта	parta
chalkboard	такта	takta
grade	баа	baa
good grade	жакшы баа	dʒakʃı baa
bad grade	жаман баа	dʒaman baa
to give a grade	баа коюу	baa kojʉu
mistake, error	ката	kata
to make mistakes	ката кетирүү	kata ketiryy
to correct (an error)	түзөтүү	tyzøtyy
cheat sheet	шпаргалка	ʃpargalka
homework	үй иши	yj iʃi
exercise (in education)	көнүгүү	kønygyy
to be present	катышуу	katıʃuu
to be absent	келбей калуу	kelbej kaluu
to miss school	сабактарды калтыруу	sabaktardı kaltıruu

to punish (vt)	жазалоо	dʒazaloo
punishment	жаза	dʒaza
conduct (behavior)	жүрүм-турум	dʒyrym-turum

report card	күндөлүк	kyndølyk
pencil	карандаш	karandaʃ
eraser	өчүргүч	øtʃyrgytʃ
chalk	бор	bor
pencil case	калем салгыч	kalem salgɪtʃ

schoolbag	портфель	portfelʲ
pen	калем сап	kalem sap
school notebook	дептер	depter
textbook	китеп	kitep
drafting compass	циркуль	tsɪrkulʲ

| to make technical drawings | чийүү | tʃijyy |
| technical drawing | чийме | tʃijme |

poem	ыр сап	ɪr sap
by heart (adv)	жатка	dʒatka
to learn by heart	жаттоо	dʒattoo

school vacation	эс алуу	es aluu
to be on vacation	эс алууда болуу	es aluuda boluu
to spend one's vacation	эс алууну өткөзүү	es aluunu øtkøzyy

test (written math ~)	текшерүү иш	tekʃeryy iʃ
essay (composition)	дил баян	dil bajan
dictation	жат жаздыруу	dʒat dʒazdɪruu
exam (examination)	экзамен	ekzamen
to take an exam	экзамен тапшыруу	ekzamen tapʃiruu
experiment (e.g., chemistry ~)	тажрыйба	tadʒrijba

95. College. University

academy	академия	akademija
university	университет	universitet
faculty (e.g., ~ of Medicine)	факультет	fakulʲtet

student (masc.)	студент бала	student bala
student (fem.)	студент кыз	student kɪz
lecturer (teacher)	мугалим	mugalim

lecture hall, room	дарскана	darskana
graduate	окуу жайды бүтүрүүчү	okuu dʒajdɪ bytyryytʃy
diploma	диплом	diplom

dissertation	диссертация	dissertatsija
study (report)	изилдөө	izildøø
laboratory	лаборатория	laboratorija

lecture	лекция	lektsija
coursemate	курсташ	kurstaʃ
scholarship	стипендия	stipendija
academic degree	илимий даража	ilimij daradʒa

96. Sciences. Disciplines

mathematics	математика	matematika
algebra	алгебра	algebra
geometry	геометрия	geometrija

astronomy	астрономия	astronomija
biology	биология	biologija
geography	география	geografija
geology	геология	geologija
history	тарых	tarıχ

medicine	медицина	meditsina
pedagogy	педагогика	pedagogika
law	укук	ukuk

physics	физика	fizika
chemistry	химия	χimija
philosophy	философия	filosofija
psychology	психология	psiχologija

97. Writing system. Orthography

grammar	грамматика	grammatika
vocabulary	лексика	leksika
phonetics	фонетика	fonetika

noun	зат атооч	zat atootʃ
adjective	сын атооч	sın atootʃ
verb	этиш	etiʃ
adverb	тактооч	taktootʃ

pronoun	ат атооч	at atootʃ
interjection	сырдык сөз	sırdık søz
preposition	препозиция	prepozitsija

root	сөздүн уңгусу	søzdyn uŋgusu
ending	жалгоо	dʒalgoo
prefix	префикс	prefiks

| syllable | муун | muun |
| suffix | суффикс | suffiks |

| stress mark | басым | basım |
| apostrophe | апостроф | apostrof |

period, dot	чекит	ʧekit
comma	үтүр	ytyr
semicolon	чекитүү үтүр	ʧekityy ytyr
colon	кош чекит	koʃ ʧekit
ellipsis	көп чекит	køp ʧekit

| question mark | суроо белгиси | suroo belgisi |
| exclamation point | илеп белгиси | ilep belgisi |

quotation marks	тырмакча	tırmakʧa
in quotation marks	тырмакчага алынган	tırmakʧaga alıngan
parenthesis	кашаа	kaʃaa
in parenthesis	кашаага алынган	kaʃaaga alıngan

hyphen	дефис	defis
dash	тире	tire
space (between words)	аралык	aralık

| letter | тамга | tamga |
| capital letter | баш тамга | baʃ tamga |

| vowel (n) | үндүү тыбыш | yndyy tıbıʃ |
| consonant (n) | үнсүз тыбыш | ynsyz tıbıʃ |

sentence	сүйлөм	syjløm
subject	сүйлөмдүн ээси	syjlømdyn eesi
predicate	баяндооч	bajandooʧ

line	сап	sap
on a new line	жаңы сап	dʒaŋı sap
paragraph	абзац	abzaʦ

word	сөз	søz
group of words	сөз айкашы	søz ajkaʃı
expression	туюнтма	tujuntma
synonym	синоним	sinonim
antonym	антоним	antonim

rule	эреже	eredʒe
exception	чектен чыгаруу	ʧekten ʧıgaruu
correct (adj)	туура	tuura

conjugation	жактоо	dʒaktoo
declension	жөндөлүш	dʒøndølyʃ
nominal case	жөндөмө	dʒøndømø
question	суроо	suroo

| to underline (vt) | баса белгилөө | basa belgiløø |
| dotted line | пунктир | punktir |

98. Foreign languages

language	тил	til
foreign (adj)	чет	tʃet
foreign language	чет тил	tʃet til
to study (vt)	окуу	okuu
to learn (language, etc.)	үйрөнүү	yjrønyy

to read (vi, vt)	окуу	okuu
to speak (vi, vt)	сүйлөө	syjløø
to understand (vt)	түшүнүү	tyʃynyy
to write (vt)	жазуу	dʒazuu

fast (adv)	тез	tez
slowly (adv)	жай	dʒaj
fluently (adv)	эркин	erkin

rules	эрежелер	eredʒeler
grammar	грамматика	grammatika
vocabulary	лексика	leksika
phonetics	фонетика	fonetika

textbook	китеп	kitep
dictionary	сөздүк	søzdyk
teach-yourself book	өзү үйрөткүч	øzy yjrøtkytʃ
phrasebook	тилачар	tilatʃar

cassette, tape	кассета	kasseta
videotape	видеокассета	videokasseta
CD, compact disc	CD, компакт-диск	sidi, kompakt-disk
DVD	DVD-диск	dividi-disk

alphabet	алфавит	alfavit
to spell (vt)	эжелеп айтуу	edʒelep ajtuu
pronunciation	айтылышы	ajtılıʃı

accent	акцент	aktsent
with an accent	акцент менен	aktsent menen
without an accent	акцентсиз	aktsentsiz

| word | сөз | søz |
| meaning | маани | maani |

course (e.g., a French ~)	курстар	kurstar
to sign up	курска жазылуу	kurska dʒazıluu
teacher	окутуучу	okutuutʃu
translation (process)	котору	kotoruu

translation (text, etc.)	котормо	kotormo
translator	котормочу	kotormoʧu
interpreter	оозеки котормочу	oozeki kotormoʧu

| polyglot | полиглот | poliglot |
| memory | эс тутум | es tutum |

Rest. Entertainment. Travel

99. Trip. Travel

tourism, travel	туризм	turizm
tourist	турист	turist
trip, voyage	саякат	sajakat
adventure	укмуштуу окуя	ukmuʃtuu okuja
trip, journey	сапар	sapar
vacation	дем алыш	dem alıʃ
to be on vacation	дем алышка чыгуу	dem alıʃka tʃıguu
rest	эс алуу	es aluu
train	поезд	poezd
by train	поезд менен	poezd menen
airplane	учак	utʃak
by airplane	учакта	utʃakta
by car	автомобилде	avtomobilde
by ship	кемеде	kemede
luggage	жүк	dʒyk
suitcase	чемодан	tʃemodan
luggage cart	араба	araba
passport	паспорт	pasport
visa	виза	viza
ticket	билет	bilet
air ticket	авиабилет	aviabilet
guidebook	жол көрсөткүч	dʒol kørsøtkytʃ
map (tourist ~)	карта	karta
area (rural ~)	жай	dʒaj
place, site	жер	dʒer
exotica (n)	экзотика	ekzotika
exotic (adj)	экзотикалуу	ekzotikaluu
amazing (adj)	ажайып	adʒajıp
group	топ	top
excursion, sightseeing tour	экскурсия	ekskursija
guide (person)	экскурсия жетекчиси	ekskursija dʒetektʃisi

100. Hotel

hotel, inn	мейманкана	mejmankana
motel	мотель	motelʲ
three-star (~ hotel)	үч жылдыздуу	ytʃ dʒɪldɪzduu
five-star	беш жылдыздуу	beʃ dʒɪldɪzduu
to stay (in a hotel, etc.)	токтоо	toktoo
room	номер	nomer
single room	бир орундуу	bir orunduu
double room	эки орундуу	eki orunduu
to book a room	номерди камдык буйрутмалоо	nomerdi kamdɪk bujrutmaloo
half board	жарым пансион	dʒarɪm pansion
full board	толук пансион	toluk pansion
with bath	ваннасы менен	vannasɪ menen
with shower	душ менен	duʃ menen
satellite television	спутник	sputnik
air-conditioner	аба желдеткич	aba dʒeldetkitʃ
towel	сүлгү	sylgy
key	ачкыч	atʃkɪtʃ
administrator	администратор	administrator
chambermaid	үй кызматкери	yj kɪzmatkeri
porter, bellboy	жүк ташуучу	dʒyk taʃuutʃu
doorman	эшик ачуучу	eʃik atʃuutʃu
restaurant	ресторан	restoran
pub, bar	бар	bar
breakfast	таңкы тамак	taŋkɪ tamak
dinner	кечки тамак	ketʃki tamak
buffet	шведче стол	ʃvedtʃe stol
lobby	вестибюль	vestibylʲ
elevator	лифт	lift
DO NOT DISTURB	ТЫНЧЫБЫЗДЫ АЛБАГЫЛА!	tɪntʃɪbɪzdɪ albagɪla!
NO SMOKING	ТАМЕКИ ЧЕГҮҮГӨ БОЛБОЙТ!	tameki tʃegyygø bolbojt!

TECHNICAL EQUIPMENT. TRANSPORTATION

Technical equipment

101. Computer

computer	компьютер	kompjʉter
notebook, laptop	ноутбук	noutbuk
to turn on	күйгүзүү	kyjgyzyy
to turn off	өчүрүү	øʧyryy
keyboard	ариптакта	ariptakta
key	баскыч	baskıʧ
mouse	чычкан	ʧıʧkan
mouse pad	килемче	kilemʧe
button	баскыч	baskıʧ
cursor	курсор	kursor
monitor	монитор	monitor
screen	экран	ekran
hard disk	катуу диск	katuu disk
hard disk capacity	катуу дисктин көлөмү	katuu disktin kølømy
memory	эс тутум	es tutum
random access memory	оперативдик эс тутум	operativdik es tutum
file	файл	fajl
folder	папка	papka
to open (vt)	ачуу	aʧuu
to close (vt)	жабуу	dʒabuu
to save (vt)	сактоо	saktoo
to delete (vt)	жок кылуу	dʒok kıluu
to copy (vt)	көчүрүү	køʧyryy
to sort (vt)	иреттөө	irettøø
to transfer (copy)	өткөрүү	øtkøryy
program	программа	programma
software	программалык	programmalık
programmer	программист	programmist
to program (vt)	программалаштыруу	programmalaʃtıruu
hacker	хакер	χaker
password	сырсөз	sırsøz

| virus | вирус | virus |
| to find, to detect | издеп табуу | izdep tabuu |

| byte | байт | bajt |
| megabyte | мегабайт | megabajt |

| data | маалыматтар | maalımattar |
| database | маалымат базасы | maalımat bazası |

cable (USB, etc.)	кабель	kabelʲ
to disconnect (vt)	ажыратуу	adʒıratuu
to connect (sth to sth)	туташтыруу	tutaʃtıruu

102. Internet. E-mail

Internet	интернет	internet
browser	браузер	brauzer
search engine	издөө аспабы	izdøø aspabı
provider	провайдер	provajder

webmaster	веб-мастер	web-master
website	веб-сайт	web-sajt
webpage	веб-баракча	web-baraktʃa

| address (e-mail ~) | дарек | darek |
| address book | дарек китепчеси | darek kiteptʃesi |

mailbox	почта ящиги	potʃta jaʃtʃigi
mail	почта	potʃta
full (adj)	толуп калган	tolup kalgan

message	кабар	kabar
incoming messages	келген кабарлар	kelgen kabarlar
outgoing messages	жөнөтүлгөн кабарлар	dʒønøtylgøn kabarlar

sender	жөнөтүүчү	dʒønøtyytʃy
to send (vt)	жөнөтүү	dʒønøtyy
sending (of mail)	жөнөтүү	dʒønøtyy

| receiver | алуучу | aluutʃu |
| to receive (vt) | алуу | aluu |

| correspondence | жазышуу | dʒazıʃuu |
| to correspond (vi) | жазышуу | dʒazıʃuu |

file	файл	fajl
to download (vt)	жүктөө	dʒyktøø
to create (vt)	жаратуу	dʒaratuu
to delete (vt)	жок кылуу	dʒok kıluu
deleted (adj)	жок кылынган	dʒok kılıngan

connection (ADSL, etc.)	байланыш	bajlanıʃ
speed	ылдамдык	ıldamdık
modem	модем	modem
access	жеткирилүү	dʒetkirilyy
port (e.g., input ~)	порт	port

| connection (make a ~) | туташуу | tutaʃuu |
| to connect to ... (vi) | ... туташуу | ... tutaʃuu |

| to select (vt) | тандоо | tandoo |
| to search (for ...) | ... издөө | ... izdøø |

103. Electricity

electricity	электр кубаты	elektr kubatı
electric, electrical (adj)	электрикалык	elektrikalık
electric power plant	электростанция	elektrostantsija
energy	энергия	energija
electric power	электр кубаты	elektr kubatı

light bulb	лампочка	lampotʃka
flashlight	шам	ʃam
street light	шам	ʃam

light	жарык	dʒarık
to turn on	күйгүзүү	kyjgyzyy
to turn off	өчүрүү	øtʃyryy
to turn off the light	жарыкты өчүрүү	dʒarıktı øtʃyryy

to burn out (vi)	күйүп кетүү	kyjyp ketyy
short circuit	кыска туташуу	kıska tutaʃuu
broken wire	үзүлүү	yzylyy
contact (electrical ~)	контакт	kontakt

light switch	өчүргүч	øtʃyrgytʃ
wall socket	розетка	rozetka
plug	сайгыч	sajgıtʃ
extension cord	узарткыч	uzartkıtʃ

fuse	эриме сактагыч	erime saktagıtʃ
cable, wire	зым	zım
wiring	электр зымы	elektr zımı

ampere	ампер	amper
amperage	токтун күчү	toktun kytʃy
volt	вольт	volʲt
voltage	чыңалуу	tʃıŋaluu

| electrical device | электр алет | elektr alet |
| indicator | көрсөткүч | kørsøtkytʃ |

electrician	электрик	elektrik
to solder (vt)	кандоо	kaŋdoo
soldering iron	кандагыч аспап	kaŋdagıtʃ aspap
electric current	электр тогу	elektr togu

104. Tools

tool, instrument	аспап	aspap
tools	аспаптар	aspaptar
equipment (factory ~)	жабдуу	dʒabduu

hammer	балка	balka
screwdriver	бурагыч	buragıtʃ
ax	балта	balta

saw	араа	araa
to saw (vt)	аралоо	araloo
plane (tool)	тактай сүргүч	taktaj syrgytʃ
to plane (vt)	сүрүү	syryy
soldering iron	кандагыч аспап	kaŋdagıtʃ aspap
to solder (vt)	кандоо	kaŋdoo

file (tool)	өгөө	øgøø
carpenter pincers	аттиш	attiʃ
lineman's pliers	жалпак тиштүү кычкач	dʒalpak tiʃtyy kıtʃkatʃ
chisel	тешкич	teʃkitʃ

drill bit	бургу	burgu
electric drill	үшкү	yʃky
to drill (vi, vt)	бургулап тешүү	burgulap teʃyy

knife	бычак	bıtʃak
pocket knife	чөнтөк бычак	tʃøntøk bıtʃak
blade	миз	miz

sharp (blade, etc.)	курч	kurtʃ
dull, blunt (adj)	мокок	mokok
to get blunt (dull)	мокотулуу	mokotuluu
to sharpen (vt)	курчутуу	kurtʃutuu

bolt	буроо	buroo
nut	бурама	burama
thread (of a screw)	бураманын сайы	buramanın sajı
wood screw	буроо мык	buroo mık

| nail | мык | mık |
| nailhead | баш | baʃ |

| ruler (for measuring) | сызгыч | sızgıtʃ |
| tape measure | рулетка | ruletka |

spirit level	деңгээл	deŋgeel
magnifying glass	чоңойтуч	tʃoŋojtutʃ
measuring instrument	ченөөчү аспап	tʃenøøtʃy aspap
to measure (vt)	ченөө	tʃenøø
scale	шкала	ʃkala
(of thermometer, etc.)		
readings	көрсөтүү ченем	kørsøtyy tʃenem
compressor	компрессор	kompressor
microscope	микроскоп	mikroskop
pump (e.g., water ~)	соргу	sorgu
robot	робот	robot
laser	лазер	lazer
wrench	гайка ачкычы	gajka atʃkɪtʃɪ
adhesive tape	жабышкак тасма	dʒabɪʃkak tasma
glue	желим	dʒelim
sandpaper	кум кагаз	kum kagaz
spring	серпилгич	serpilgitʃ
magnet	магнит	magnit
gloves	колкап	kolkap
rope	аркан	arkan
cord	жип	dʒip
wire (e.g., telephone ~)	зым	zɪm
cable	кабель	kabelʲ
sledgehammer	барскан	barskan
prybar	лом	lom
ladder	шаты	ʃatɪ
stepladder	кичинекей шаты	kitʃinekej ʃatɪ
to screw (tighten)	бурап бекитүү	burap bekityy
to unscrew (lid, filter, etc.)	бурап чыгаруу	burap tʃɪgaruu
to tighten	кысуу	kɪsuu
(e.g., with a clamp)		
to glue, to stick	жабыштыруу	dʒabɪʃtɪruu
to cut (vt)	кесүү	kesyy
malfunction (fault)	бузулгандык	buzulgandɪk
repair (mending)	оңдоо	oŋdoo
to repair, to fix (vt)	оңдоо	oŋdoo
to adjust (machine, etc.)	тууралоо	tuuraloo
to check (to examine)	текшерүү	tekʃeryy
checking	текшерүү	tekʃeryy
readings	көрсөтүү ченем	kørsøtyy tʃenem
reliable, solid (machine)	ишеничтүү	iʃenitʃtyy
complex (adj)	кыйын	kɪjɪn

to rust (get rusted)	**дат басуу**	dat basuu
rusty, rusted (adj)	**дат баскан**	dat baskan
rust	**дат**	dat

Transportation

105. Airplane

airplane	учак	uʧak
air ticket	авиабилет	aviabilet
airline	авиакомпания	aviakompanija
airport	аэропорт	aeroport
supersonic (adj)	сверхзвуковой	sverχzvukovoj
captain	кеме командири	keme komandiri
crew	экипаж	ekipadʒ
pilot	учкуч	uʧkuʧ
flight attendant (fem.)	стюардесса	stɯardessa
navigator	штурман	ʃturman
wings	канаттар	kanattar
tail	куйрук	kujruk
cockpit	кабина	kabina
engine	кыймылдаткыч	kɯjmɯldatkɯʧ
undercarriage (landing gear)	шасси	ʃassi
turbine	турбина	turbina
propeller	пропеллер	propeller
black box	кара куту	kara kutu
yoke (control column)	штурвал	ʃturval
fuel	күйүүчү май	kyjyyʧy may
safety card	коопсуздук көрсөтмөсү	koopsuzduk kørsøtmøsy
oxygen mask	кислород чүмбөтү	kislorod ʧymbøty
uniform	бир беткей кийим	bir betkey kijim
life vest	куткарууучу күрмө	kutkaruuʧu kyrmø
parachute	парашют	paraʃɯt
takeoff	учуп көтөрүлүү	uʧup køtørylyy
to take off (vi)	учуп көтөрүлүү	uʧup køtørylyy
runway	учуп чыгуу тилкеси	uʧup ʧɯguu tilkesi
visibility	көрүнүш	kørynyʃ
flight (act of flying)	учуу	uʧuu
altitude	бийиктик	bijiktik
air pocket	аба чүңкуру	aba ʧyŋkuru
seat	орун	orun
headphones	кулакчын	kulakʧɯn

folding tray (tray table)	бүктөлмө стол	byktølmø stol
airplane window	иллюминатор	illuminator
aisle	өтмөк	øtmøk

106. Train

train	поезд	poezd
commuter train	электричка	elektritʃka
express train	бат жүрүүчү поезд	bat dʒyryytʃy poezd
diesel locomotive	тепловоз	teplovoz
steam locomotive	паровоз	parovoz

| passenger car | вагон | vagon |
| dining car | вагон-ресторан | vagon-restoran |

rails	рельсалар	relʲsalar
railroad	темир жолу	temir dʒolu
railway tie	шпала	ʃpala

platform (railway ~)	платформа	platforma
track (~ 1, 2, etc.)	жол	dʒol
semaphore	семафор	semafor
station	бекет	beket

engineer (train driver)	машинист	maʃinist
porter (of luggage)	жук ташуучу	dʒuk taʃuutʃu
car attendant	проводник	provodnik
passenger	жүргүнчү	dʒyrgyntʃy
conductor (ticket inspector)	текшерүүчү	tekʃeryytʃy

| corridor (in train) | коридор | koridor |
| emergency brake | стоп-кран | stop-kran |

compartment	купе	kupe
berth	текче	tektʃe
upper berth	үстүңкү текче	ystyŋky tektʃe
lower berth	ылдыйкы текче	ıldıjkı tektʃe
bed linen, bedding	жууркан-төшөк	dʒuurkan-tøʃøk

ticket	билет	bilet
schedule	ырааттама	ıraattama
information display	табло	tablo

to leave, to depart	жөнөө	dʒønøø
departure (of train)	жөнөө	dʒønøø
to arrive (ab. train)	келүү	kelyy
arrival	келүү	kelyy
to arrive by train	поезд менен келүү	poezd menen kelyy
to get on the train	поездге отуруу	poezdge oturuu

to get off the train	поездден түшүү	poezdden tyſyy
train wreck	кыйроо	kijroo
to derail (vi)	рельсадан чыгып кетүү	rel'sadan ʧɪgɪp ketyy

steam locomotive	паровоз	parovoz
stoker, fireman	от жагуучу	ot dʒaguuʧu
firebox	меш	meʃ
coal	көмүр	kømyr

107. Ship

| ship | кеме | keme |
| vessel | кеме | keme |

steamship	пароход	paroxod
riverboat	теплоход	teploxod
cruise ship	лайнер	lajner
cruiser	крейсер	krejser

yacht	яхта	jaxta
tugboat	буксир	buksir
barge	баржа	bardʒa
ferry	паром	parom

| sailing ship | парус | parus |
| brigantine | бригантина | brigantina |

| ice breaker | муз жаргыч кеме | muz dʒargɪʧ keme |
| submarine | суу астында жүрүүчү кеме | suu astında dʒyryyʧy keme |

boat (flat-bottomed ~)	кайык	kajık
dinghy	шлюпка	ʃlʉpka
lifeboat	куткаруу шлюпкасы	kutkaruu ʃlʉpkası
motorboat	катер	kater

captain	капитан	kapitan
seaman	матрос	matros
sailor	деңизчи	deŋizʧi
crew	экипаж	ekipadʒ

boatswain	боцман	botsman
ship's boy	юнга	jʉnga
cook	кок	kok
ship's doctor	кеме доктуру	keme dokturu

deck	палуба	paluba
mast	мачта	matʃta
sail	парус	parus
hold	трюм	trʉm

bow (prow)	тумшук	tumʃuk
stern	кеменин арткы бөлүгү	kemenin artkı bølygy
oar	калак	kalak
screw propeller	винт	vint
cabin	каюта	kajʉta
wardroom	кают-компания	kajʉt-kompanija
engine room	машина бөлүгү	maʃina bølygy
bridge	капитан мостиги	kapitan mostigi
radio room	радиорубка	radiorubka
wave (radio)	толкун	tolkun
logbook	кеме журналы	keme dʒurnalı
spyglass	дүрбү	dyrby
bell	коңгуроо	koŋguroo
flag	байрак	bajrak
hawser (mooring ~)	аркан	arkan
knot (bowline, etc.)	түйүн	tyjyn
deckrails	туткуч	tutkutʃ
gangway	трап	trap
anchor	кеме казык	keme kazık
to weigh anchor	кеме казыкты көтөрүү	keme kazıktı køtøryy
to drop anchor	кеме казыкты таштоо	keme kazıktı taʃtoo
anchor chain	казык чынжыры	kazık tʃındʒırı
port (harbor)	порт	port
quay, wharf	причал	pritʃal
to berth (moor)	келип токтоо	kelip toktoo
to cast off	жээктен алыстоо	dʒeekten alıstoo
trip, voyage	саякат	sajakat
cruise (sea trip)	деңиз саякаты	deŋiz sajakatı
course (route)	курс	kurs
route (itinerary)	каттам	kattam
fairway (safe water channel)	фарватер	farvater
shallows	тайыз жер	tajız dʒer
to run aground	тайыз жерге отуруу	tajız dʒerge oturuu
storm	бороон чапкын	boroon tʃapkın
signal	сигнал	signal
to sink (vi)	чөгүү	tʃøgyy
Man overboard!	Сууда адам бар!	suuda adam bar!
SOS (distress signal)	SOS	sos
ring buoy	куткаруучу тегерек	kutkaruutʃu tegerek

108. Airport

airport	аэропорт	aeroport
airplane	учак	uʧak
airline	авиакомпания	aviakompanija
air traffic controller	авиадиспетчер	aviadispetʧer
departure	учуп кетүү	uʧup ketyy
arrival	учуп келүү	uʧup kelyy
to arrive (by plane)	учуп келүү	uʧup kelyy
departure time	учуп кетүү убактысы	uʧup ketyy ubaktısı
arrival time	учуп келүү убактысы	uʧup kelyy ubaktısı
to be delayed	кармалуу	karmaluu
flight delay	учуп кетүүнүн кечигиши	uʧup ketyynyn ketʃigiʃi
information board	маалымат таблосу	maalımat tablosu
information	маалымат	maalımat
to announce (vt)	кулактандыруу	kulaktandıruu
flight (e.g., next ~)	рейс	rejs
customs	бажыкана	badʒıkana
customs officer	бажы кызматкери	badʒı kızmatkeri
customs declaration	бажы декларациясы	badʒı deklaratsijası
to fill out (vt)	толтуруу	tolturuu
to fill out the declaration	декларация толтуруу	deklaratsija tolturuu
passport control	паспорт текшерүү	pasport tekʃeryy
luggage	жүк	dʒyk
hand luggage	кол жүгү	kol dʒygy
luggage cart	араба	araba
landing	конуу	konuu
landing strip	конуу тилкеси	konuu tilkesi
to land (vi)	конуу	konuu
airstair (passenger stair)	трап	trap
check-in	катталуу	kattaluu
check-in counter	каттоо стойкасы	kattoo stojkası
to check-in (vi)	катталуу	kattaluu
boarding pass	отуруу үчүн талон	oturuu yʧyn talon
departure gate	чыгуу	ʧıguu
transit	транзит	tranzit
to wait (vt)	күтүү	kytyy
departure lounge	күтүү залы	kytyy zalı
to see off	узатуу	uzatuu
to say goodbye	коштошуу	koʃtoʃuu

Life events

109. Holidays. Event

celebration, holiday	майрам	majram
national day	улуттук	uluttuk
public holiday	майрам күнү	majram kyny
to commemorate (vt)	майрамдоо	majramdoo
event (happening)	окуя	okuja
event (organized activity)	иш-чара	iʃ-tʃara
banquet (party)	банкет	banket
reception (formal party)	кабыл алуу	kabıl aluu
feast	той	toj
anniversary	жылдык	dʒıldık
jubilee	юбилей	jʉbilej
to celebrate (vt)	белгилөө	belgiløø
New Year	Жаны жыл	dʒanı dʒıl
Happy New Year!	Жаны Жылыңар менен!	dʒanı dʒılıŋar menen!
Santa Claus	Аяз ата, Санта Клаус	ajaz ata, santa klaus
Christmas	Рождество	rodʒdestvo
Merry Christmas!	Рождество майрамыңыз менен!	rodʒdestvo majramıŋız menen!
Christmas tree	Жаңы жылдык балаты	dʒaŋı dʒıldık balatı
fireworks (fireworks show)	салют	salʉt
wedding	үйлөнүү той	yjlønyy toy
groom	күйөө	kyjøø
bride	колукту	koluktu
to invite (vt)	чакыруу	tʃakıruu
invitation card	чакыруу	tʃakıruu
guest	конок	konok
to visit (~ your parents, etc.)	конокко баруу	konokko baruu
to meet the guests	конок тосуу	konok tosuu
gift, present	белек	belek
to give (sth as present)	белек берүү	belek beryy
to receive gifts	белек алуу	belek aluu
bouquet (of flowers)	десте	deste
congratulations	куттуктоо	kuttuktoo

to congratulate (vt)	куттуктоо	kuttuktoo
greeting card	куттуктоо ачык каты	kuttuktoo atʃık katı
to send a postcard	ачык катты жөнөтүү	atʃık kattı dʒønøtyy
to get a postcard	ачык катты алуу	atʃık kattı aluu

toast	каалоо тилек	kaaloo tilek
to offer (a drink, etc.)	ооз тийгизүү	ooz tijgizyy
champagne	шампан	ʃampan

to enjoy oneself	көңүл ачуу	køŋyl atʃuu
merriment (gaiety)	көңүлдүүлүк	køŋyldyylyk
joy (emotion)	кубаныч	kubanıtʃ

| dance | бий | bij |
| to dance (vi, vt) | бийлөө | bijløø |

| waltz | вальс | valʲs |
| tango | танго | tango |

110. Funerals. Burial

cemetery	мүрзө	myrzø
grave, tomb	мүрзө	myrzø
cross	крест	krest
gravestone	мүрзө үстүндөгү жазуу	myrzø ystyndøgy dʒazuu
fence	тосмо	tosmo
chapel	кичинекей чиркөө	kitʃinekej tʃirkøø

death	өлүм	ølym
to die (vi)	өлүү	ølyy
the deceased	маркум	markum
mourning	аза	aza

to bury (vt)	көмүү	kømyy
funeral home	ырасым бюросу	ırasım bʉrosu
funeral	сөөк узатуу жана көмүү	søøk uzatuu dʒana kømyy

| wreath | гүлчамбар | gyltʃambar |
| casket, coffin | табыт | tabıt |

| hearse | катафалк | katafalk |
| shroud | кепин | kepin |

funeral procession	узатуу жүрүшү	uzatuu dʒyryʃy
funerary urn	сөөк күлдүн кутусу	søøk kyldyn kutusu
crematory	крематорий	krematorij

obituary	некролог	nekrolog
to cry (weep)	ыйлоо	ıjloo
to sob (vi)	боздоп ыйлоо	bozdop ıjloo

111. War. Soldiers

platoon	взвод	vzvod
company	рота	rota
regiment	полк	polk
army	армия	armija
division	дивизия	divizija
section, squad	отряд	otrʲad
host (army)	куралдуу аскер	kuralduu asker
soldier	аскер	asker
officer	офицер	ofitser
private	катардагы жоокер	katardagı dʒooker
sergeant	сержант	serdʒant
lieutenant	лейтенант	lejtenant
captain	капитан	kapitan
major	майор	major
colonel	полковник	polkovnik
general	генерал	general
sailor	деңизчи	deŋiztʃi
captain	капитан	kapitan
boatswain	боцман	botsman
artilleryman	артиллерист	artillerist
paratrooper	десантник	desantnik
pilot	учкуч	utʃkutʃ
navigator	штурман	ʃturman
mechanic	механик	meχanik
pioneer (sapper)	сапёр	sapʲor
parachutist	парашютист	paraʃutist
reconnaissance scout	чалгынчы	tʃalgıntʃı
sniper	көзатар	køzatar
patrol (group)	жол-күзөт	dʒol-kyzøt
to patrol (vt)	жол-күзөткө чыгуу	dʒol-kyzøtkø tʃıguu
sentry, guard	сакчы	saktʃı
warrior	жоокер	dʒooker
patriot	мекенчил	mekentʃil
hero	баатыр	baatır
heroine	баатыр айым	baatır ajım
traitor	чыккынчы	tʃıkkıntʃı
to betray (vt)	кыянаттык кылуу	kıjanattık kıluu
deserter	качкын	katʃkın
to desert (vi)	качуу	katʃuu

mercenary	жалданма	dʒaldanma
recruit	жаңы алынган аскер	dʒaŋɯ alɯngan asker
volunteer	ыктыярчы	ɯktɯjartʃɯ

dead (n)	өлтүрүлгөн	øltyrylgøn
wounded (n)	жарадар	dʒaradar
prisoner of war	туткун	tutkun

112. War. Military actions. Part 1

war	согуш	soguʃ
to be at war	согушуу	soguʃuu
civil war	жарандык согуш	dʒarandɯk soguʃ

treacherously (adv)	жүзү каралык менен кол салуу	dʒyzy karalɯk menen kol saluu
declaration of war	согушту жарыялоо	soguʃtu dʒarɯjaloo
to declare (~ war)	согуш жарыялоо	soguʃ dʒarɯjaloo
aggression	агрессия	agressija
to attack (invade)	кол салуу	kol saluu

to invade (vt)	басып алуу	basɯp aluu
invader	баскынчы	baskɯntʃɯ
conqueror	басып алуучу	basɯp aluutʃu

defense	коргонуу	korgonuu
to defend (a country, etc.)	коргоо	korgoo
to defend (against ...)	коргонуу	korgonuu

enemy	душман	duʃman
foe, adversary	каршылаш	karʃɯlaʃ
enemy (as adj)	душмандын	duʃmandɯn

| strategy | стратегия | strategija |
| tactics | тактика | taktika |

order	буйрук	bujruk
command (order)	команда	komanda
to order (vt)	буйрук берүү	bujruk beryy
mission	тапшырма	tapʃɯrma
secret (adj)	жашыруун	dʒaʃɯruun

battle	салгылаш	salgɯlaʃ
battle	согуш	soguʃ
combat	салгылаш	salgɯlaʃ

attack	чабуул	tʃabuul
charge (assault)	чабуул	tʃabuul
to storm (vt)	чабуул жасоо	tʃabuul dʒasoo
siege (to be under ~)	тегеректеп курчоо	tegerektep kurtʃoo

| offensive (n) | чабуул | tʃabuul |
| to go on the offensive | чабуул салуу | tʃabuul saluu |

| retreat | чегинүү | tʃeginyy |
| to retreat (vi) | чегинүү | tʃeginyy |

| encirclement | курчоо | kurtʃoo |
| to encircle (vt) | курчоого алуу | kurtʃoogo aluu |

bombing (by aircraft)	бомба жаадыруу	bomba dʒaadıruu
to drop a bomb	бомба таштоо	bomba taʃtoo
to bomb (vt)	бомба жаадыруу	bomba dʒaadıruu
explosion	жарылуу	dʒarıluu

shot	атылуу	atıluu
to fire (~ a shot)	атуу	atuu
firing (burst of ~)	атуу	atuu

to aim (to point a weapon)	мээлөө	meeløø
to point (a gun)	мээлөө	meeløø
to hit (the target)	тийүү	tijyy

to sink (~ a ship)	чөктүрүү	tʃøktyryy
hole (in a ship)	тешик	teʃik
to founder, to sink (vi)	суу астына кетүү	suu astına ketyy

front (war ~)	майдан	majdan
evacuation	эвакуация	evakuatsija
to evacuate (vt)	эвакуациялоо	evakuatsijaloo

trench	окоп	okop
barbwire	тикендүү зым	tikendyy zım
barrier (anti tank ~)	тосмо	tosmo
watchtower	мунара	munara

military hospital	госпиталь	gospitalʲ
to wound (vt)	жарадар кылуу	dʒaradar kıluu
wound	жара	dʒara
wounded (n)	жарадар	dʒaradar
to be wounded	жаракат алуу	dʒarakat aluu
serious (wound)	оор жаракат	oor dʒarakat

113. War. Military actions. Part 2

captivity	туткун	tutkun
to take captive	туткунга алуу	tutkunga aluu
to be held captive	туткунда болуу	tutkunda boluu
to be taken captive	туткунга түшүү	tutkunga tyʃyy
concentration camp	концлагерь	kontslagerʲ
prisoner of war	туткун	tutkun

to escape (vi)	качуу	katʃuu
to betray (vt)	кыянаттык кылуу	kıjanattık kıluu
betrayer	чыккынчы	tʃıkkıntʃı
betrayal	чыккынчылык	tʃıkkıntʃılık
to execute (by firing squad)	атып өлтүрүү	atıp øltyryy
execution (by firing squad)	атып өлтүрүү	atıp øltyryy
equipment (military gear)	аскер кийими	asker kijimi
shoulder board	погон	pogon
gas mask	противогаз	protivogaz
field radio	рация	ratsija
cipher, code	шифр	ʃifr
secrecy	жекеликте сактоо	dʒekelikte saktoo
password	сырсөз	sırsøz
land mine	мина	mina
to mine (road, etc.)	миналоо	minaloo
minefield	мина талаасы	mina talaası
air-raid warning	аба айгайы	aba ajgajı
alarm (alert signal)	айгай	ajgaj
signal	сигнал	signal
signal flare	сигнал ракетасы	signal raketası
headquarters	штаб	ʃtab
reconnaissance	чалгын	tʃalgın
situation	кырдаал	kırdaal
report	рапорт	raport
ambush	буктурма	bukturma
reinforcement (of army)	кошумча күч	koʃumtʃa kytʃ
target	бута	buta
proving ground	полигон	poligon
military exercise	манервлер	manervler
panic	дүрбөлөң	dyrbøløŋ
devastation	кыйроо	kıjroo
destruction, ruins	кыйроо	kıjroo
to destroy (vt)	кыйратуу	kıjratuu
to survive (vi, vt)	тирүү калуу	tiryy kaluu
to disarm (vt)	куралсыздандыруу	kuralsızdandıruu
to handle (~ a gun)	мамиле кылуу	mamile kıluu
Attention!	Түз тур!	tyz tur!
At ease!	Эркин!	erkin!
feat, act of courage	эрдик	erdik
oath (vow)	ант	ant

to swear (an oath)	ант берүү	ant beryy
decoration (medal, etc.)	сыйлык	sıjlık
to award (give medal to)	сыйлоо	sıjloo
medal	медаль	medalʲ
order (e.g., ~ of Merit)	орден	orden

victory	жеңиш	dʒeɲiʃ
defeat	жеңилүү	dʒeɲilyy
armistice	жарашуу	dʒaraʃuu

standard (battle flag)	байрак	bajrak
glory (honor, fame)	даңк	daŋk
parade	парад	parad
to march (on parade)	маршта басуу	marʃta basuu

114. Weapons

weapons	курал	kural
firearms	курал жарак	kural dʒarak
cold weapons (knives, etc.)	атылбас курал	atılbas kural

chemical weapons	химиялык курал	χimijalık kural
nuclear (adj)	ядерлүү	jaderlyy
nuclear weapons	ядерлүү курал	jaderlyy kural

| bomb | бомба | bomba |
| atomic bomb | атом бомбасы | atom bombası |

pistol (gun)	тапанча	tapantʃa
rifle	мылтык	mıltık
submachine gun	автомат	avtomat
machine gun	пулемёт	pulemʲot

muzzle	мылтыктын оозу	mıltıktın oozu
barrel	ствол	stvol
caliber	калибр	kalibr

trigger	курок	kurok
sight (aiming device)	кароолго алуу	karoolgo aluu
magazine	магазин	magazin
butt (shoulder stock)	күндак	kyndak

| hand grenade | граната | granata |
| explosive | жарылуучу зат | dʒarıluutʃu zat |

bullet	ок	ok
cartridge	патрон	patron
charge	дүрмөк	dyrmøk
ammunition	ок-дары	ok-darı

bomber (aircraft)	бомбалоочу	bombalootʃu
fighter	кыйраткыч учак	kıjratkıtʃ utʃak
helicopter	вертолёт	vertolʲot

anti-aircraft gun	зенитка	zenitka
tank	танк	tank
tank gun	замбирек	zambirek

artillery	артиллерия	artillerija
gun (cannon, howitzer)	замбирек	zambirek
to lay (a gun)	мээлөө	meeløø

shell (projectile)	снаряд	snarʲad
mortar bomb	мина	mina
mortar	миномёт	minomʲot
splinter (shell fragment)	сыныктар	sınıktar

submarine	суу астында жүрүүчү кеме	suu astında dʒyryytʃy keme
torpedo	торпеда	torpeda
missile	ракета	raketa

to load (gun)	октоо	oktoo
to shoot (vi)	атуу	atuu
to point at (the cannon)	мээлөө	meeløø
bayonet	найза	najza

rapier	шпага	ʃpaga
saber (e.g., cavalry ~)	кылыч	kılıtʃ
spear (weapon)	найза	najza
bow	жаа	dʒaa
arrow	жебе	dʒebe
musket	мушкет	muʃket
crossbow	арбалет	arbalet

115. Ancient people

primitive (prehistoric)	алгачкы	algatʃkı
prehistoric (adj)	тарыхтан илгери	tarıxtan ilgeri
ancient (~ civilization)	байыркы	bajırkı

Stone Age	Таш доору	taʃ dooru
Bronze Age	Коло доору	kolo dooru
Ice Age	Муз доору	muz dooru

tribe	уруу	uruu
cannibal	адам жегич	adam dʒegitʃ
hunter	аңчы	aŋtʃı
to hunt (vi, vt)	аңчылык кылуу	aŋtʃılık kıluu
mammoth	мамонт	mamont

cave	үңкүр	yŋkyr
fire	от	ot
campfire	от	ot
cave painting	ташка чегерилген сүрөт	taʃka ʧegerilgen syrøt

tool (e.g., stone ax)	эмгек куралы	emgek kuralı
spear	найза	najza
stone ax	таш балта	taʃ balta
to be at war	согушуу	soguʃuu
to domesticate (vt)	колго көндүрүү	kolgo køndyryy

idol	бут	but
to worship (vt)	сыйынуу	sıjınuu
superstition	жок нерсеге ишенүү	dʒok nersege iʃenyy
rite	ырым-жырым	ırım-dʒırım

evolution	эволюция	evolʉtsija
development	өнүгүү	ønygyy
disappearance (extinction)	жок болуу	dʒok boluu
to adapt oneself	ылайыкташуу	ılajıktaʃuu

archeology	археология	arχeologija
archeologist	археолог	arχeolog
archeological (adj)	археологиялык	arχeologijalık

excavation site	казуу жери	kazuu dʒeri
excavations	казуу иштери	kazuu iʃteri
find (object)	табылга	tabılga
fragment	фрагмент	fragment

116. Middle Ages

people (ethnic group)	эл	el
peoples	элдер	elder
tribe	уруу	uruu
tribes	уруулар	uruular

barbarians	варварлар	varvarlar
Gauls	галлдар	galldar
Goths	готтор	gottor
Slavs	славяндар	slavʲandar
Vikings	викингдер	vikingder

| Romans | римдиктер | rimdikter |
| Roman (adj) | римдик | rimdik |

Byzantines	византиялыктар	vizantijalıktar
Byzantium	Византия	vizantija
Byzantine (adj)	византиялык	vizantijalık
emperor	император	imperator

leader, chief (tribal ~)	башчы	baʃtʃı
powerful (~ king)	кудуреттүү	kudurettyy
king	король, падыша	korolʲ, padıʃa
ruler (sovereign)	башкаруучу	baʃkaruutʃu

knight	рыцарь	rıtsarʲ
feudal lord	феодал	feodal
feudal (adj)	феодалдуу	feodalduu
vassal	вассал	vassal

duke	герцог	gertsog
earl	граф	graf
baron	барон	baron
bishop	епископ	episkop

armor	курал жана соот-шайман	kural dʒana soot-ʃajman
shield	калкан	kalkan
sword	кылыч	kılıtʃ
visor	туулганын бет калканы	tuulganın bet kalkanı
chainmail	зоот	zoot

| Crusade | крест астындагы черүү | krest astındagı tʃeryy |
| crusader | черүүге чыгуучу | tʃeryygø tʃıguutʃu |

territory	аймак	ajmak
to attack (invade)	кол салуу	kol saluu
to conquer (vt)	ээ болуу	ee boluu
to occupy (invade)	басып алуу	basıp aluu

siege (to be under ~)	тегеректеп курчоо	tegerektep kurtʃoo
besieged (adj)	курчалган	kurtʃalgan
to besiege (vt)	курчоого алуу	kurtʃoogo aluu

inquisition	инквизиция	inkvizitsija
inquisitor	инквизитор	inkvizitor
torture	кыйноо	kıjnoo
cruel (adj)	ырайымсыз	ırajımsız
heretic	еретик	eretik
heresy	ересь	eresʲ

seafaring	деңизде сүзүү	deŋizde syzyy
pirate	деңиз каракчысы	deŋiz karaktʃısı
piracy	деңиз каракчылыгы	deŋiz karaktʃılıgı
boarding (attack)	абордаж	abordadʒ
loot, booty	олжо	oldʒo
treasures	казына	kazına

discovery	ачылыш	atʃılıʃ
to discover (new land, etc.)	таап ачуу	taap atʃuu
expedition	экспедиция	ekspeditsija
musketeer	мушкетёр	muʃketʲor

cardinal	кардинал	kardinal
heraldry	геральдика	geralʲdika
heraldic (adj)	гералдык	geraldık

117. Leader. Chief. Authorities

king	король, падыша	korolʲ, padıʃa
queen	ханыша	χanıʃa
royal (adj)	падышалык	padıʃalık
kingdom	падышалык	padıʃalık

| prince | канзаада | kanzaada |
| princess | ханбийке | χanbijke |

president	президент	prezident
vice-president	вице-президент	viʦe-prezident
senator	сенатор	senator
monarch	монарх	monarχ
ruler (sovereign)	башкаруучу	baʃkaruuʧu
dictator	диктатор	diktator
tyrant	зулум	zulum
magnate	магнат	magnat

director	директор	direktor
chief	башчы	baʃʧı
manager (director)	башкаруучу	baʃkaruuʧu
boss	шеф	ʃef
owner	кожоюн	koʤoʤʉn
leader	алдыңкы катардагы	aldıŋkı katardagı
head (~ of delegation)	башчы	baʃʧı
authorities	бийликтер	bijlikter
superiors	башчылар	baʃʧılar

governor	губернатор	gubernator
consul	консул	konsul
diplomat	дипломат	diplomat
mayor	мэр	mer
sheriff	шериф	ʃerif

emperor	император	imperator
tsar, czar	падыша	padıʃa
pharaoh	фараон	faraon
khan	хан	χan

118. Breaking the law. Criminals. Part 1

| bandit | ууру-кески | uuru-keski |
| crime | кылмыш | kılmıʃ |

criminal (person)	кылмышкер	kılmıʃker
thief	ууру	uuru
to steal (vi, vt)	уурдоо	uurdoo
stealing (larceny)	уруулук	uruuluk
theft	уурдоо	uurdoo

to kidnap (vt)	ала качуу	ala katʃuu
kidnapping	ала качуу	ala katʃuu
kidnapper	ала качуучу	ala katʃuutʃu

ransom	кутказуу акчасы	kutkazuu aktʃası
to demand ransom	кутказуу акчага талап коюу	kutkazuu aktʃaga talap kojʉu

to rob (vt)	тоноо	tonoo
robbery	тоноо	tonoo
robber	тоноочу	tonootʃu

to extort (vt)	опузалоо	opuzaloo
extortionist	опузалоочу	opuzalootʃu
extortion	опуза	opuza

to murder, to kill	өлтүрүү	øltyryy
murder	өлтүрүү	øltyryy
murderer	киши өлтүргүч	kiʃi øltyrgytʃ

gunshot	атылуу	atıluu
to fire (~ a shot)	атуу	atuu
to shoot to death	атып салуу	atıp saluu
to shoot (vi)	атуу	atuu
shooting	атышуу	atıʃuu

incident (fight, etc.)	окуя	okuja
fight, brawl	уруш	uruʃ
Help!	Жардамга!	dʒardamga!
victim	жапа чеккен	dʒapa tʃekken

to damage (vt)	зыян келтирүү	zıjan keltiryy
damage	залал	zalal
dead body, corpse	өлүк	ølyk
grave (~ crime)	оор	oor

to attack (vt)	кол салуу	kol saluu
to beat (to hit)	уруу	uruu
to beat up	ур-токмокко алуу	ur-tokmokko aluu
to take (rob of sth)	тартып алуу	tartıp aluu
to stab to death	союп өлтүрүү	sojʉp øltyryy
to maim (vt)	майып кылуу	majıp kıluu
to wound (vt)	жарадар кылуу	dʒaradar kıluu

blackmail	шантаж кылуу	ʃantadʒ kıluu
to blackmail (vt)	шантаждоо	ʃantadʒdoo

blackmailer	шантажист	ʃantadʒist
protection racket	рэкет	reket
racketeer	рэкетир	reketir
gangster	гангстер	gangster
mafia, Mob	мафия	mafija

pickpocket	чөнтөк ууру	tʃøntøk uuru
burglar	бузуп алуучу ууру	buzup aluutʃu uuru
smuggling	контрабанда	kontrabanda
smuggler	контрабандачы	kontrabandatʃı

forgery	окшотуп жасоо	okʃotup dʒasoo
to forge (counterfeit)	жасалмалоо	dʒasalmaloo
fake (forged)	жасалма	dʒasalma

119. Breaking the law. Criminals. Part 2

rape	зордуктоо	zorduktoo
to rape (vt)	зордуктоо	zorduktoo
rapist	зордукчул	zorduktʃul
maniac	маньяк	manjak

prostitute (fem.)	сойку	sojku
prostitution	сойкучулук	sojkutʃuluk
pimp	жак бакты	dʒak baktı

| drug addict | баңги | baŋgi |
| drug dealer | баңгизат сатуучу | baŋgizat satuutʃu |

to blow up (bomb)	жардыруу	dʒardıruu
explosion	жарылуу	dʒarıluu
to set fire	өрттөө	ørttøø
arsonist	өрттөөчү	ørttøøtʃy

terrorism	терроризм	terrorizm
terrorist	террорист	terrorist
hostage	заложник	zalodʒnik

to swindle (deceive)	алдоо	aldoo
swindle, deception	алдамчылык	aldamtʃılık
swindler	алдамчы	aldamtʃı

to bribe (vt)	сатып алуу	satıp aluu
bribery	сатып алуу	satıp aluu
bribe	пара	para

poison	уу	uu
to poison (vt)	ууландыруу	uulandıruu
to poison oneself	уулануу	uulanuu
suicide (act)	жанын кыюю	dʒanın kıdʒuu

suicide (person)	жанын кыйгыч	dʒanın kıjgıtʃ
to threaten (vt)	коркутуу	korkutuu
threat	коркунуч	korkunutʃ
to make an attempt	кол салуу	kol saluu
attempt (attack)	кол салуу	kol saluu
to steal (a car)	айдап кетүү	ajdap ketyy
to hijack (a plane)	ала качуу	ala katʃuu
revenge	кек	kek
to avenge (get revenge)	өч алуу	øtʃ aluu
to torture (vt)	кыйноо	kıjnoo
torture	кыйноо	kıjnoo
to torment (vt)	азапка салуу	azapka saluu
pirate	деңиз каракчысы	deŋiz karaktʃısı
hooligan	бейбаш	bejbaʃ
armed (adj)	куралданган	kuraldangan
violence	зордук	zorduk
illegal (unlawful)	мыйзамдан тыш	mıjzamdan tıʃ
spying (espionage)	тыңчылык	tıŋtʃılık
to spy (vi)	тыңчылык кылуу	tıŋtʃılık kıluu

120. Police. Law. Part 1

justice	адилеттүү сот	adilettyy sot
court (see you in ~)	сот	sot
judge	сот	sot
jurors	сот калыстары	sot kalıstarı
jury trial	калыстар соту	sot
to judge, to try (vt)	сотко тартуу	sotko tartuu
lawyer, attorney	жактоочу	dʒaktootʃu
defendant	сот жообуна тартылган киши	sot dʒoobuna tartılgan kiʃi
dock	соттуулар отуруучу орун	sottuular oturuutʃu orun
charge	айыптоо	ajıptoo
accused	айыпталуучу	ajıptaluutʃu
sentence	өкүм	økym
to sentence (vt)	өкүм чыгаруу	økym tʃıgaruu
guilty (culprit)	күнөөкөр	kynøøkør
to punish (vt)	жазалоо	dʒazaloo
punishment	жаза	dʒaza

fine (penalty)	айып	ajıp
life imprisonment	өмүр бою	ømyr bojʉ
death penalty	өлүм жазасы	ølym dʒazası
electric chair	электр столу	elektr stolu
gallows	дарга	darga

| to execute (vt) | өлүм жазасын аткаруу | ølym dʒazasın atkaruu |
| execution | өлүм жазасын аткаруу | ølym dʒazasın atkaruu |

| prison, jail | түрмө | tyrmø |
| cell | камера | kamera |

escort (convoy)	конвой	konvoj
prison guard	түрмө сакчысы	tyrmø saktʃısı
prisoner	камактагы адам	kamaktagı adam

| handcuffs | кишен | kiʃen |
| to handcuff (vt) | кишен кийгизүү | kiʃen kijgizyy |

prison break	качуу	katʃuu
to break out (vi)	качуу	katʃuu
to disappear (vi)	жоголуп кетүү	dʒogolup ketyy
to release (from prison)	бошотуу	boʃotuu
amnesty	амнистия	amnistija

police	полиция	politsija
police officer	полиция кызматкери	politsija kızmatkeri
police station	полиция бөлүмү	politsija bølymy
billy club	резина союлчасы	rezina sojʉltʃası
bullhorn	керней	kernej

patrol car	жол күзөт машинасы	dʒol kyzøt maʃinası
siren	сирена	sirena
to turn on the siren	сиренаны басуу	sirenanı basuu
siren call	сиренанын боздошу	sirenanın bozdoʃu

crime scene	кылмыш болгон жер	kılmıʃ bolgon dʒer
witness	күбө	kybø
freedom	эркиндик	erkindik
accomplice	шерик	ʃerik
to flee (vi)	из жашыруу	iz dʒaʃıruu
trace (to leave a ~)	из	iz

121. Police. Law. Part 2

search (investigation)	издөө	izdøø
to look for ...	... издөө	... izdøø
suspicion	шек	ʃek
suspicious (e.g., ~ vehicle)	шектүү	ʃektyy
to stop (cause to halt)	токтотуу	toktotuu

to detain (keep in custody)	кармоо	karmoo
case (lawsuit)	иш	iʃ
investigation	териштирүү	teriʃtiryy
detective	аңдуучу	aŋduutʃu
investigator	тергөөчү	tergøøtʃy
hypothesis	жоромол	dʒoromol

motive	себеп	sebep
interrogation	сурак	surak
to interrogate (vt)	суракка алуу	surakka aluu
to question (~ neighbors, etc.)	сураштыруу	suraʃtıruu
check (identity ~)	текшерүү	tekʃeryy

round-up (raid)	тегеректөө	tegerektøø
search (~ warrant)	тинтүү	tintyy
chase (pursuit)	куу	kuu
to pursue, to chase	изине түшүү	izine tyʃyy
to track (a criminal)	изине түшүү	izine tyʃyy

arrest	камак	kamak
to arrest (sb)	камакка алуу	kamakka aluu
to catch (thief, etc.)	кармоо	karmoo
capture	колго түшүрүү	kolgo tyʃyryy

document	документ	dokument
proof (evidence)	далил	dalil
to prove (vt)	далилдөө	dalildøø
footprint	из	iz
fingerprints	манжанын изи	mandʒanın izi
piece of evidence	далил	dalil

alibi	алиби	alibi
innocent (not guilty)	бейкүнөө	bejkynøø
injustice	адилетсиздик	adiletsizdik
unjust, unfair (adj)	адилетсиз	adiletsiz

criminal (adj)	кылмыштуу	kılmıʃtuu
to confiscate (vt)	тартып алуу	tartıp aluu
drug (illegal substance)	баңгизат	baŋgizat
weapon, gun	курал	kural
to disarm (vt)	куралсыздандыруу	kuralsızdandıruu

to order (command)	буйрук берүү	bujruk beryy
to disappear (vi)	жоголуп кетүү	dʒogolup ketyy

law	мыйзам	mıjzam
legal, lawful (adj)	мыйзамдуу	mıjzamduu
illegal, illicit (adj)	мыйзамдан тыш	mıjzamdan tıʃ

responsibility (blame)	жоопкерчилик	dʒoopkertʃilik
responsible (adj)	жоопкерчиликтүү	dʒoopkertʃiliktyy

NATURE

The Earth. Part 1

122. Outer space

space	космос	kosmos
space (as adj)	космос	kosmos
outer space	космос мейкиндиги	kosmos mejkindigi
world	дүйнө	dyjnø
universe	аалам	aalam
galaxy	галактика	galaktika
star	жылдыз	dʒıldız
constellation	жылдыздар	dʒıldızdar
planet	планета	planeta
satellite	жолдош	dʒoldoʃ
meteorite	метеорит	meteorit
comet	комета	kometa
asteroid	астероид	asteroid
orbit	орбита	orbita
to revolve (~ around the Earth)	айлануу	ajlanuu
atmosphere	атмосфера	atmosfera
the Sun	күн	kyn
solar system	күн системасы	kyn sisteması
solar eclipse	күндүн тутулушу	kyndyn tutuluʃu
the Earth	Жер	dʒer
the Moon	Ай	aj
Mars	Марс	mars
Venus	Венера	venera
Jupiter	Юпитер	jʉpiter
Saturn	Сатурн	saturn
Mercury	Меркурий	merkurij
Uranus	Уран	uran
Neptune	Нептун	neptun
Pluto	Плутон	pluton
Milky Way	Саманчынын жолу	samantʃının dʒolu

| Great Bear (Ursa Major) | Чоң Жетиген | tʃoŋ dʒetigen |
| North Star | Полярдык Жылдыз | polʲardık dʒıldız |

Martian	марсианин	marsianin
extraterrestrial (n)	инопланетянин	inoplanetʲanin
alien	келгин	kelgin
flying saucer	учуучу табак	utʃuutʃu tabak

spaceship	космос кемеси	kosmos kemesi
space station	орбитадагы станция	orbitadagı stantsija
blast-off	старт	start

engine	кыймылдаткыч	kıjmıldatkıtʃ
nozzle	сопло	soplo
fuel	күйүүчү май	kyjyytʃy may

cockpit, flight deck	кабина	kabina
antenna	антенна	antenna
porthole	иллюминатор	illɯminator
solar panel	күн батареясы	kyn batarejası
spacesuit	скафандр	skafandr

| weightlessness | салмаксыздык | salmaksızdık |
| oxygen | кислород | kislorod |

| docking (in space) | жалгаштыруу | dʒalgaʃtıruu |
| to dock (vi, vt) | жалгаштыруу | dʒalgaʃtıruu |

observatory	обсерватория	observatorija
telescope	телескоп	teleskop
to observe (vt)	байкоо	bajkoo
to explore (vt)	изилдее	izildøø

123. The Earth

the Earth	Жер	dʒer
the globe (the Earth)	жер шары	dʒer ʃarı
planet	планета	planeta

atmosphere	атмосфера	atmosfera
geography	география	geografija
nature	табийгат	tabijgat

globe (table ~)	глобус	globus
map	карта	karta
atlas	атлас	atlas

Europe	Европа	evropa
Asia	Азия	azija
Africa	Африка	afrika

Australia	Австралия	avstralija
America	Америка	amerika
North America	Северная Америка	severnaja amerika
South America	Южная Америка	jʉdʒnaja amerika

| Antarctica | Антарктида | antarktida |
| the Arctic | Арктика | arktika |

124. Cardinal directions

north	түндүк	tyndyk
to the north	түндүккө	tyndykkø
in the north	түндүктө	tyndyktø
northern (adj)	түндүк	tyndyk

south	түштүк	tyʃtyk
to the south	түштүккө	tyʃtykkø
in the south	түштүктө	tyʃtyktø
southern (adj)	түштүк	tyʃtyk

west	батыш	batıʃ
to the west	батышка	batıʃka
in the west	батышта	batıʃta
western (adj)	батыш	batıʃ

east	чыгыш	tʃıgıʃ
to the east	чыгышка	tʃıgıʃka
in the east	чыгышта	tʃıgıʃta
eastern (adj)	чыгыш	tʃıgıʃ

125. Sea. Ocean

sea	деңиз	deŋiz
ocean	мухит	muχit
gulf (bay)	булуң	buluŋ
straits	кысык	kısık

| land (solid ground) | жер | dʒer |
| continent (mainland) | материк | materik |

island	арал	aral
peninsula	жарым арал	dʒarım aral
archipelago	архипелаг	arχipelag

bay, cove	булуң	buluŋ
harbor	гавань	gavanʲ
lagoon	лагуна	laguna
cape	тумшук	tumʃuk

137

atoll	атолл	atoll
reef	риф	rif
coral	маржан	marʤan
coral reef	маржан рифи	marʤan rifi
deep (adj)	терең	tereŋ
depth (deep water)	терेңдик	tereŋdik
abyss	түбү жок	tyby ʤok
trench (e.g., Mariana ~)	ойдуң	ojduŋ
current (Ocean ~)	агым	agım
to surround (bathe)	курчап туруу	kurʧap turuu
shore	жээк	ʤeek
coast	жээк	ʤeek
flow (flood tide)	суунун көтөрүлүшү	suunun køtørylyʃy
ebb (ebb tide)	суунун тартылуусу	suunun tartıluusu
shoal	тайыздык	tajızdık
bottom (~ of the sea)	суунун түбү	suunun tyby
wave	толкун	tolkun
crest (~ of a wave)	толкундун кыры	tolkundun kırı
spume (sea foam)	көбүк	købyk
storm (sea storm)	бороон чапкын	boroon ʧapkın
hurricane	бороон	boroon
tsunami	цунами	tsunami
calm (dead ~)	штиль	ʃtilʲ
quiet, calm (adj)	тынч	tınʧ
pole	уюл	ujʉl
polar (adj)	полярдык	polʲardık
latitude	кеңдик	keŋdik
longitude	узундук	uzunduk
parallel	параллель	parallelʲ
equator	экватор	ekvator
sky	асман	asman
horizon	горизонт	gorizont
air	аба	aba
lighthouse	маяк	majak
to dive (vi)	сүңгүү	syŋgyy
to sink (ab. boat)	чөгүп кетүү	ʧøgyp ketyy
treasures	казына	kazına

126. Seas' and Oceans' names

Atlantic Ocean	Атлантика мухити	atlantika muχiti
Indian Ocean	Индия мухити	indija muχiti

| Pacific Ocean | Тынч мухити | tıntʃ muχiti |
| Arctic Ocean | Түндүк Муз мухити | tyndyk muz muχiti |

Black Sea	Кара деңиз	kara deŋiz
Red Sea	Кызыл деңиз	kızıl deŋiz
Yellow Sea	Сары деңиз	sarı deŋiz
White Sea	Ак деңиз	ak deŋiz

Caspian Sea	Каспий деңизи	kaspij deŋizi
Dead Sea	Өлүк деңиз	ølyk deŋiz
Mediterranean Sea	Жер Ортолук деңиз	dʒer ortoluk deŋiz

| Aegean Sea | Эгей деңизи | egej deŋizi |
| Adriatic Sea | Адриатика деңизи | adriatika deŋizi |

Arabian Sea	Аравия деңизи	aravija deŋizi
Sea of Japan	Япон деңизи	japon deŋizi
Bering Sea	Беринг деңизи	bering deŋizi
South China Sea	Түштүк-Кытай деңизи	tyʃtyk-kıtaj deŋizi

Coral Sea	Маржан деңизи	mardʒan deŋizi
Tasman Sea	Тасман деңизи	tasman deŋizi
Caribbean Sea	Кариб деңизи	karib deŋizi

| Barents Sea | Баренц деңизи | barents deŋizi |
| Kara Sea | Карск деңизи | karsk deŋizi |

North Sea	Түндүк деңиз	tyndyk deŋiz
Baltic Sea	Балтика деңизи	baltika deŋizi
Norwegian Sea	Норвегиялык деңизи	norvegijalık deŋizi

127. Mountains

mountain	тоо	too
mountain range	тоо тизмеги	too tizmegi
mountain ridge	тоо кыркалары	too kırkaları

summit, top	чоку	tʃoku
peak	чоку	tʃoku
foot (~ of the mountain)	тоо этеги	too etegi
slope (mountainside)	эңкейиш	eŋkejiʃ

volcano	вулкан	vulkan
active volcano	күйүп жаткан	kyjyp dʒatkan
dormant volcano	өчүп калган вулкан	øtʃyp kalgan vulkan

eruption	атырылып чыгуу	atırılıp tʃıguu
crater	кратер	krater
magma	магма	magma
lava	лава	lava

molten (~ lava)	кызыган	kızıgan
canyon	каньон	kanʲon
gorge	капчыгай	kaptʃɪgaj
crevice	жарака	dʒaraka
abyss (chasm)	жар	dʒar

pass, col	ашуу	aʃuu
plateau	дөңсөө	døŋsøø
cliff	зоока	zooka
hill	дөбө	døbø

glacier	муз	muz
waterfall	шаркыратма	ʃarkɪratma
geyser	гейзер	gejzer
lake	көл	køl

plain	түздүк	tyzdyk
landscape	теребел	terebel
echo	жаңырык	dʒaŋɪrɪk

alpinist	альпинист	alʲpinist
rock climber	скалолаз	skalolaz
to conquer (in climbing)	багындыруу	bagɪndɪruu
climb (an easy ~)	тоонун чокусуна чыгуу	toonun tʃokusuna tʃɪguu

128. Mountains names

The Alps	Альп тоолору	alʲp tooloru
Mont Blanc	Монблан	monblan
The Pyrenees	Пиреней тоолору	pirenej tooloru

The Carpathians	Карпат тоолору	karpat tooloru
The Ural Mountains	Урал тоолору	ural tooloru
The Caucasus Mountains	Кавказ тоолору	kavkaz tooloru
Mount Elbrus	Эльбрус	elʲbrus

The Altai Mountains	Алтай тоолору	altaj tooloru
The Tian Shan	Тянь-Шань	tjanʲ-ʃanʲ
The Pamir Mountains	Памир тоолору	pamir tooloru
The Himalayas	Гималай тоолору	gimalaj tooloru
Mount Everest	Эверест	everest
The Andes	Анд тоолору	and tooloru
Mount Kilimanjaro	Килиманджаро	kilimandʒaro

129. Rivers

| river | дарыя | darɪja |
| spring (natural source) | булак | bulak |

riverbed (river channel)	сай	saj
basin (river valley)	бассейн	bassejn
to flow into …	… куюу	… kujɯu
tributary	куйма	kujma
bank (of river)	жээк	ʤeek
current (stream)	агым	agım
downstream (adv)	агым боюнча	agım bojɯnʧa
upstream (adv)	агымга каршы	agımga karʃı
inundation	ташкын	taʃkın
flooding	суу ташкыны	suu taʃkını
to overflow (vi)	дайранын ташышы	dajranın taʃıʃı
to flood (vt)	суу каптоо	suu kaptoo
shallow (shoal)	тайыздык	tajızdık
rapids	босого	bosogo
dam	тогоон	togoon
canal	канал	kanal
reservoir (artificial lake)	суу сактагыч	suu saktagıʧ
sluice, lock	шлюз	ʃlɯz
water body (pond, etc.)	көлмө	kølmø
swamp (marshland)	саз	saz
bog, marsh	баткак	batkak
whirlpool	айлампа	ajlampa
stream (brook)	суу	suu
drinking (ab. water)	ичилчү суу	iʧilʧy suu
fresh (~ water)	тузсуз	tuzsuz
ice	муз	muz
to freeze over (ab. river, etc.)	тоңуп калуу	toɲup kaluu

130. Rivers' names

Seine	Сена	sena
Loire	Луара	luara
Thames	Темза	temza
Rhine	Рейн	rejn
Danube	Дунай	dunaj
Volga	Волга	volga
Don	Дон	don
Lena	Лена	lena
Yellow River	Хуанхэ	χuanχe

Yangtze	Янцзы	janʦzɪ
Mekong	Меконг	mekong
Ganges	Ганг	gang

Nile River	Нил	nil
Congo River	Конго	kongo
Okavango River	Оканго	okavango
Zambezi River	Замбези	zambezi
Limpopo River	Лимпопо	limpopo
Mississippi River	Миссисипи	missisipi

131. Forest

| forest, wood | токой | tokoj |
| forest (as adj) | токойлуу | tokojluu |

thick forest	чытырман токой	ʧɪtɪrman tokoj
grove	токойчо	tokojʧo
forest clearing	аянт	ajant

| thicket | бадал | badal |
| scrubland | бадал | badal |

| footpath (troddenpath) | чыйыр жол | ʧɪjɪr ʤol |
| gully | жар | ʤar |

tree	дарак	darak
leaf	жалбырак	ʤalbɪrak
leaves (foliage)	жалбырак	ʤalbɪrak

fall of leaves	жалбырак түшүү мезгили	ʤalbɪrak tyʃyy mezgili
to fall (ab. leaves)	түшүү	tyʃyy
top (of the tree)	чоку	ʧoku

branch	бутак	butak
bough	бутак	butak
bud (on shrub, tree)	бүчүр	byʧyr
needle (of pine tree)	ийне	ijne
pine cone	тобурчак	toburʧak

tree hollow	көңдөй	køŋdøj
nest	уя	uja
burrow (animal hole)	ийин	ijin
trunk	сеңгек	søŋgøk
root	тамыр	tamɪr
bark	кыртыш	kɪrtɪʃ
moss	мох	moχ
to uproot (remove trees or tree stumps)	дүмүрүн казуу	dymyryn kazuu

to chop down	кыюу	kıjʉu
to deforest (vt)	токойду кыюу	tokojdu kıjʉu
tree stump	дүмүр	dymyr

campfire	от	ot
forest fire	өрт	ørt
to extinguish (vt)	өчүрүү	øtʃyryy

forest ranger	токойчу	tokojtʃu
protection	өсүмдүктөрдү коргоо	øsymdyktørdy korgoo
to protect (~ nature)	сактоо	saktoo
poacher	браконьер	brakonjer
steel trap	капкан	kapkan

to pick (mushrooms)	терүү	teryy
to pick (berries)	терүү	teryy
to lose one's way	адашып кетүү	adaʃıp ketyy

132. Natural resources

natural resources	жаратылыш байлыктары	dʒaratılıʃ bajlıktarı
minerals	пайдалуу кендер	pajdaluu kender
deposits	кен	ken
field (e.g., oilfield)	кендүү жер	kendyy dʒer

to mine (extract)	казуу	kazuu
mining (extraction)	казуу	kazuu
ore	кен	ken
mine (e.g., for coal)	шахта	ʃaχta
shaft (mine ~)	шахта	ʃaχta
miner	кенчи	kentʃi

| gas (natural ~) | газ | gaz |
| gas pipeline | газопровод | gazoprovod |

oil (petroleum)	мунайзат	munajzat
oil pipeline	мунайзар түтүгү	munajzar tytygy
oil well	мунайзат скважинасы	munajzat skvadʒinası
derrick (tower)	мунайзат мунарасы	munajzat munarası
tanker	танкер	tanker

sand	кум	kum
limestone	акиташ	akitaʃ
gravel	шагыл	ʃagıl
peat	торф	torf
clay	ылай	ılaj
coal	көмүр	kømyr
iron (ore)	темир	temir
gold	алтын	altın

silver	күмүш	kymyʃ
nickel	никель	nikelʲ
copper	жез	dʒez

zinc	цинк	tsɪnk
manganese	марганец	marganeʦ
mercury	сымап	sɪmap
lead	коргошун	korgoʃun

mineral	минерал	mineral
crystal	кристалл	kristall
marble	мрамор	mramor
uranium	уран	uran

The Earth. Part 2

133. Weather

weather	аба-ырайы	aba-ırajı
weather forecast	аба-ырайы боюнча маалымат	aba-ırajı bojunʧa maalımat
temperature	температура	temperatura
thermometer	термометр	termometr
barometer	барометр	barometr
humid (adj)	нымдуу	nımduu
humidity	ным	nım
heat (extreme ~)	ысык	ısık
hot (torrid)	кыйын ысык	kıjın ısık
it's hot	ысык	ısık
it's warm	жылуу	dʒıluu
warm (moderately hot)	жылуу	dʒıluu
it's cold	суук	suuk
cold (adj)	суук	suuk
sun	күн	kyn
to shine (vi)	күн тийүү	kyn tijyy
sunny (day)	күн ачык	kyn atʃık
to come up (vi)	чыгуу	ʧıguu
to set (vi)	батуу	batuu
cloud	булут	bulut
cloudy (adj)	булуттуу	buluttuu
rain cloud	булут	bulut
somber (gloomy)	күн бүркөк	kyn byrkøk
rain	жамгыр	dʒamgır
it's raining	жамгыр жаап жатат	dʒamgır dʒaap dʒatat
rainy (~ day, weather)	жаандуу	dʒaanduu
to drizzle (vi)	дыбыратуу	dıbıratuu
pouring rain	нөшөрлөгөн жаан	nøʃørløgøn dʒaan
downpour	нөшөр	nøʃør
heavy (e.g., ~ rain)	катуу	katuu
puddle	көлчүк	køltʃyk
to get wet (in rain)	суу болуу	suu boluu
fog (mist)	туман	tuman

foggy	тумандуу	tumanduu
snow	кар	kar
it's snowing	кар жаап жатат	kar ʤaap ʤatat

134. Severe weather. Natural disasters

thunderstorm	чагылгандуу жаан	ʧagılganduu ʤaan
lightning (~ strike)	чагылган	ʧagılgan
to flash (vi)	жарк этүү	ʤark etyy

thunder	күн күркүрөө	kyn kyrkyrøø
to thunder (vi)	күн күркүрөө	kyn kyrkyrøø
it's thundering	күн күркүрөп жатат	kyn kyrkyrøp ʤatat

| hail | мөндүр | møndyr |
| it's hailing | мөндүр түшүп жатат | møndyr tyʃyp ʤatat |

| to flood (vt) | суу каптоо | suu kaptoo |
| flood, inundation | ташкын | taʃkın |

earthquake	жер титирөө	ʤer titirøø
tremor, shoke	жердин силкиниши	ʤerdin silkiniʃi
epicenter	эпицентр	epitsentr

| eruption | атырылып чыгуу | atırılıp ʧıguu |
| lava | лава | lava |

twister	куюн	kujʉn
tornado	торнадо	tornado
typhoon	тайфун	tajfun

hurricane	бороон	boroon
storm	бороон чапкын	boroon ʧapkın
tsunami	цунами	tsunami

cyclone	циклон	tsıklon
bad weather	жаан-чачындуу күн	ʤaan-ʧaʧınduu kyn
fire (accident)	өрт	ørt
disaster	кыйроо	kıjroo
meteorite	метеорит	meteorit

avalanche	көчкү	køʧky
snowslide	кар көчкүсү	kar køʧkysy
blizzard	кар бороону	kar boroonu
snowstorm	бурганак	burganak

Fauna

135. Mammals. Predators

predator	жырткыч	ʤɪrtkɪʧ
tiger	жолборс	ʤolbors
lion	арстан	arstan
wolf	карышкыр	karɪʃkɪr
fox	түлкү	tylky
jaguar	ягуар	jaguar
leopard	леопард	leopard
cheetah	гепард	gepard
black panther	пантера	pantera
puma	пума	puma
snow leopard	илбирс	ilbirs
lynx	сүлөөсүн	syløøsyn
coyote	койот	kojot
jackal	чөө	ʧøø
hyena	гиена	giena

136. Wild animals

animal	жаныбар	ʤanıbar
beast (animal)	жапайы жаныбар	ʤapajı ʤanıbar
squirrel	тыйын чычкан	tıjın ʧıʧkan
hedgehog	кирпичечен	kirpiʧeʧen
hare	коен	koen
rabbit	коен	koen
badger	кашкулак	kaʃkulak
raccoon	енот	enot
hamster	хомяк	χomʲak
marmot	суур	suur
mole	момолой	momoloj
mouse	чычкан	ʧıʧkan
rat	келемиш	kelemiʃ
bat	жарганат	ʤarganat
ermine	арс чычкан	ars ʧıʧkan
sable	киш	kiʃ

marten	суусар	suusar
weasel	ласка	laska
mink	норка	norka

| beaver | кемчет | kemʧet |
| otter | кундуз | kunduz |

horse	жылкы	ʤɪlkɪ
moose	багыш	bagɪʃ
deer	бугу	bugu
camel	төө	tøø

bison	бизон	bizon
wisent	зубр	zubr
buffalo	буйвол	bujvol

zebra	зебра	zebra
antelope	антилопа	antilopa
roe deer	элик	elik
fallow deer	лань	lanʲ
chamois	жейрен	ʤejren
wild boar	каман	kaman

whale	кит	kit
seal	тюлень	tʉlenʲ
walrus	морж	morʤ
fur seal	деңиз мышыгы	deŋiz mɪʃɪgɪ
dolphin	дельфин	delʲfin

bear	аюу	ajʉu
polar bear	ак аюу	ak ajʉu
panda	панда	panda

monkey	маймыл	majmɪl
chimpanzee	шимпанзе	ʃimpanze
orangutan	орангутанг	orangutang
gorilla	горилла	gorilla
macaque	макака	makaka
gibbon	гиббон	gibbon

elephant	пил	pil
rhinoceros	керик	kerik
giraffe	жираф	ʤiraf
hippopotamus	бегемот	begemot

| kangaroo | кенгуру | kenguru |
| koala (bear) | коала | koala |

mongoose	мангуст	mangust
chinchilla	шиншилла	ʃinʃilla
skunk	скунс	skuns
porcupine	чүткөр	ʧʏtkør

137. Domestic animals

cat	ургаачы мышык	urgaatʃı mıʃık
tomcat	эркек мышык	erkek mıʃık
dog	ит	it
horse	жылкы	dʒılkı
stallion (male horse)	айгыр	ajgır
mare	бээ	bee
cow	уй	uj
bull	бука	buka
ox	өгүз	øgyz
sheep (ewe)	кой	koj
ram	кочкор	kotʃkor
goat	эчки	etʃki
billy goat, he-goat	теке	teke
donkey	эшек	eʃek
mule	качыр	katʃır
pig, hog	чочко	tʃotʃko
piglet	торопой	toropoj
rabbit	коен	koen
hen (chicken)	тоок	took
rooster	короз	koroz
duck	өрдөк	ørdøk
drake	эркек өрдөк	erkek ørdøk
goose	каз	kaz
tom turkey, gobbler	күрп	kyrp
turkey (hen)	ургаачы күрп	urgaatʃı kyrp
domestic animals	үй жаныбарлары	yj dʒanıbarları
tame (e.g., ~ hamster)	колго үйрөтүлгөн	kolgo yjrøtylgøn
to tame (vt)	колго үйрөтүү	kolgo yjrøtyy
to breed (vt)	өстүрүү	østyryy
farm	ферма	ferma
poultry	үй канаттулары	yj kanattuları
cattle	мал	mal
herd (cattle)	бада	bada
stable	аткана	atkana
pigpen	чочкокана	tʃotʃkokana
cowshed	уйкана	ujkana
rabbit hutch	коенкана	koenkana
hen house	тоокана	tookana

138. Birds

bird	куш	kuʃ
pigeon	көгүчкөн	køgytʃkøn
sparrow	таранчы	tarantʃı
tit (great tit)	синица	sinitsa
magpie	сагызган	sagızgan
raven	кузгун	kuzgun
crow	карга	karga
jackdaw	таан	taan
rook	чаркарга	tʃarkarga
duck	өрдөк	ørdøk
goose	каз	kaz
pheasant	кыргоол	kırgool
eagle	бүркүт	byrkyt
hawk	ителги	itelgi
falcon	шумкар	ʃumkar
vulture	жору	dʒoru
condor (Andean ~)	кондор	kondor
swan	аккуу	akkuu
crane	турна	turna
stork	илегилек	ilegilek
parrot	тотукуш	totukuʃ
hummingbird	колибри	kolibri
peacock	тоос	toos
ostrich	төө куш	tøø kuʃ
heron	көк кытан	køk kıtan
flamingo	фламинго	flamingo
pelican	биргазан	birgazan
nightingale	булбул	bulbul
swallow	чабалекей	tʃabalekej
thrush	таркылдак	tarkıldak
song thrush	сайрагыч таркылдак	sajragıtʃ tarkıldak
blackbird	кара таңдай таркылдак	kara taŋdaj tarkıldak
swift	кардыгач	kardıgatʃ
lark	торгой	torgoj
quail	бөдөнө	bødønø
woodpecker	тоңкулдак	toŋkuldak
cuckoo	күкүк	kykyk
owl	мыкый үкү	mıkıj yky
eagle owl	үкү	yky

wood grouse	керең кур	kereŋ kur
black grouse	кара кур	kara kur
partridge	кекилик	kekilik
starling	чыйырчык	ʧɪjɪrʧɪk
canary	канарейка	kanarejka
hazel grouse	токой чили	tokoj ʧili
chaffinch	зяблик	zʲablik
bullfinch	снегирь	snegirʲ
seagull	ак чардак	ak ʧardak
albatross	альбатрос	alʲbatros
penguin	пингвин	pingvin

139. Fish. Marine animals

bream	лещ	leʃʧ
carp	карп	karp
perch	окунь	okunʲ
catfish	жаян	dʒajan
pike	чортон	ʧorton
salmon	лосось	lososʲ
sturgeon	осётр	osʲotr
herring	сельдь	selʲdʲ
Atlantic salmon	сёмга	sʲomga
mackerel	скумбрия	skumbrija
flatfish	камбала	kambala
zander, pike perch	судак	sudak
cod	треска	treska
tuna	тунец	tunets
trout	форель	forelʲ
eel	угорь	ugorʲ
electric ray	скат	skat
moray eel	мурена	murena
piranha	пиранья	piranja
shark	акула	akula
dolphin	дельфин	delʲfin
whale	кит	kit
crab	краб	krab
jellyfish	медуза	meduza
octopus	сегиз бут	segiz but
starfish	деңиз жылдызы	deŋiz dʒɪldɪzɪ
sea urchin	деңиз кирписи	deŋiz kirpisi

seahorse	деңиз тайы	deŋiz tajı
oyster	устрица	ustritsa
shrimp	креветка	krevetka
lobster	омар	omar
spiny lobster	лангуст	langust

140. Amphibians. Reptiles

snake	жылан	dʒılan
venomous (snake)	уулуу	uuluu

viper	кара чаар жылан	kara tʃaar dʒılan
cobra	кобра	kobra
python	питон	piton
boa	удав	udav

grass snake	сары жылан	sarı dʒılan
rattle snake	шакылдак жылан	ʃakıldak dʒılan
anaconda	анаконда	anakonda

lizard	кескелдирик	keskeldirik
iguana	игуана	iguana
monitor lizard	эчкемер	etʃkemer
salamander	саламандра	salamandra
chameleon	хамелеон	χameleon
scorpion	чаян	tʃajan

turtle	ташбака	taʃbaka
frog	бака	baka
toad	курбака	kurbaka
crocodile	крокодил	krokodil

141. Insects

insect, bug	курт-кумурска	kurt-kumurska
butterfly	көпөлөк	køpøløk
ant	кумурска	kumurska
fly	чымын	tʃımın
mosquito	чиркей	tʃirkej
beetle	коңуз	koŋuz

wasp	аары	aarı
bee	бал аары	bal aarı
bumblebee	жапан аары	dʒapan aarı
gadfly (botfly)	көгөөн	køgøøn

spider	жөргөмүш	dʒørgømyʃ
spiderweb	желе	dʒele

dragonfly	ийнелик	ijnelik
grasshopper	чегиртке	ʧegirtke
moth (night butterfly)	көпөлөк	køpøløk

cockroach	таракан	tarakan
tick	кене	kene
flea	бүргө	byrgø
midge	майда чымын	majda ʧımın

locust	чегиртке	ʧegirtke
snail	үлүл	ylyl
cricket	кара чегиртке	kara ʧegirtke
lightning bug	жалтырак коңуз	dʒaltırak koŋuz
ladybug	айланкөчөк	ajlankøʧøk
cockchafer	саратан коңуз	saratan koŋuz

leech	сүлүк	sylyk
caterpillar	каз таман	kaz taman
earthworm	жер курту	dʒer kurtu
larva	курт	kurt

Flora

142. Trees

tree	дарак	darak
deciduous (adj)	жалбырактуу	dʒalbıraktuu
coniferous (adj)	ийне жалбырактуулар	ijne dʒalbıraktuular
evergreen (adj)	дайым жашыл	dajım dʒaʃıl
apple tree	алма бак	alma bak
pear tree	алмурут бак	almurut bak
sweet cherry tree	гилас	gilas
sour cherry tree	алча	altʃa
plum tree	кара өрүк	kara øryk
birch	ак кайың	ak kajıŋ
oak	эмен	emen
linden tree	жөкө дарак	dʒøkø darak
aspen	бай терек	baj terek
maple	клён	klʲon
spruce	кара карагай	kara karagaj
pine	карагай	karagaj
larch	лиственница	listvennitsa
fir tree	пихта	piχta
cedar	кедр	kedr
poplar	терек	terek
rowan	четин	tʃetin
willow	мажүрүм тал	madʒyrym tal
alder	ольха	olʲχa
beech	бук	buk
elm	кара жыгач	kara dʒıgatʃ
ash (tree)	ясень	jasenʲ
chestnut	каштан	kaʃtan
magnolia	магнолия	magnolija
palm tree	пальма	palʲma
cypress	кипарис	kiparis
mangrove	мангро дарагы	mangro daragı
baobab	баобаб	baobab
eucalyptus	эвкалипт	evkalipt
sequoia	секвойя	sekvoja

143. Shrubs

bush	бадал	badal
shrub	бадал	badal
grapevine	жүзүм	dʒyzym
vineyard	жүзүмдүк	dʒyzymdyk
raspberry bush	дан куурай	dan kuuraj
blackcurrant bush	кара карагат	kara karagat
redcurrant bush	кызыл карагат	kızıl karagat
gooseberry bush	крыжовник	krıdʒovnik
acacia	акация	akatsija
barberry	бөрү карагат	børy karagat
jasmine	жасмин	dʒasmin
juniper	кара арча	kara artʃa
rosebush	роза бадалы	roza badalı
dog rose	ит мурун	it murun

144. Fruits. Berries

fruit	мөмө-жемиш	mømø-dʒemiʃ
fruits	мөмө-жемиш	mømø-dʒemiʃ
apple	алма	alma
pear	алмурут	almurut
plum	кара өрүк	kara øryk
strawberry (garden ~)	кулпунай	kulpunaj
sour cherry	алча	altʃa
sweet cherry	гилас	gilas
grape	жүзүм	dʒyzym
raspberry	дан куурай	dan kuuraj
blackcurrant	кара карагат	kara karagat
redcurrant	кызыл карагат	kızıl karagat
gooseberry	крыжовник	krıdʒovnik
cranberry	клюква	klʉkva
orange	апельсин	apelʲsin
mandarin	мандарин	mandarin
pineapple	ананас	ananas
banana	банан	banan
date	курма	kurma
lemon	лимон	limon
apricot	өрүк	øryk

peach	шабдаалы	ʃabdaalı
kiwi	киви	kivi
grapefruit	грейпфрут	grejpfrut

berry	жер жемиш	dʒer dʒemiʃ
berries	жер жемиштер	dʒer dʒemiʃter
cowberry	брусника	brusnika
wild strawberry	кызылгат	kızılgat
bilberry	кара моюл	kara mojʉl

145. Flowers. Plants

| flower | гүл | gүl |
| bouquet (of flowers) | десте | deste |

rose (flower)	роза	roza
tulip	жоогазын	dʒoogazın
carnation	гвоздика	gvozdika
gladiolus	гладиолус	gladiolus

cornflower	ботокөз	botokøz
harebell	коңгуроо гүл	koŋguroo gүl
dandelion	каакым-кукум	kaakım-kukum
camomile	ромашка	romaʃka

aloe	алоэ	aloe
cactus	кактус	kaktus
rubber plant, ficus	фикус	fikus

lily	лилия	lilija
geranium	герань	geranʲ
hyacinth	гиацинт	giatsint

mimosa	мимоза	mimoza
narcissus	нарцисс	nartsiss
nasturtium	настурция	nasturtsija

orchid	орхидея	orχideja
peony	пион	pion
violet	бинапша	binapʃa

pansy	алагүл	alagүl
forget-me-not	незабудка	nezabudka
daisy	маргаритка	margaritka

poppy	кызгалдак	kızgaldak
hemp	наша	naʃa
mint	жалбыз	dʒalbız
lily of the valley	ландыш	landıʃ
snowdrop	байчечекей	bajtʃetʃekej

nettle	чалкан	tʃalkan
sorrel	ат кулак	at kulak
water lily	чөмүч баш	tʃømytʃ baʃ
fern	папоротник	paporotnik
lichen	лишайник	liʃajnik
conservatory (greenhouse)	күнөскана	kynøskana
lawn	газон	gazon
flowerbed	клумба	klumba
plant	өсүмдүк	øsymdyk
grass	чөп	tʃøp
blade of grass	бир тал чөп	bir tal tʃøp
leaf	жалбырак	dʒalbırak
petal	гүлдүн желекчеси	gyldyn dʒelektʃesi
stem	сабак	sabak
tuber	жемиш тамыр	dʒemiʃ tamır
young plant (shoot)	өсмө	øsmø
thorn	тикен	tiken
to blossom (vi)	гүлдөө	gyldøø
to fade, to wither	соолуу	sooluu
smell (odor)	жыт	dʒıt
to cut (flowers)	кесүү	kesyy
to pick (a flower)	үзүү	yzyy

146. Cereals, grains

grain	дан	dan
cereal crops	дан эгиндери	dan eginderi
ear (of barley, etc.)	машак	maʃak
wheat	буудай	buudaj
rye	кара буудай	kara buudaj
oats	сулу	sulu
millet	таруу	taruu
barley	арпа	arpa
corn	жүгөрү	dʒygøry
rice	күрүч	kyrytʃ
buckwheat	гречиха	gretʃixa
pea plant	нокот	nokot
kidney bean	төө буурчак	tøø buurtʃak
soy	соя	soja
lentil	жасмык	dʒasmık
beans (pulse crops)	буурчак	buurtʃak

COUNTRIES. NATIONALITIES

147. Western Europe

Europe	Европа	evropa
European Union	Европа Биримдиги	evropa birimdigi
Austria	Австрия	avstrija
Great Britain	Улуу Британия	uluu britanija
England	Англия	anglija
Belgium	Бельгия	belʹgija
Germany	Германия	germanija
Netherlands	Нидерланддар	niderlanddar
Holland	Голландия	gollandija
Greece	Греция	gretsija
Denmark	Дания	danija
Ireland	Ирландия	irlandija
Iceland	Исландия	islandija
Spain	Испания	ispanija
Italy	Италия	italija
Cyprus	Кипр	kipr
Malta	Мальта	malʹta
Norway	Норвегия	norvegija
Portugal	Португалия	portugalija
Finland	Финляндия	finlʹandija
France	Франция	frantsija
Sweden	Швеция	ʃvetsija
Switzerland	Швейцария	ʃvejtsarija
Scotland	Шотландия	ʃotlandija
Vatican	Ватикан	vatikan
Liechtenstein	Лихтенштейн	liχtenʃtejn
Luxembourg	Люксембург	lʉksemburg
Monaco	Монако	monako

148. Central and Eastern Europe

Albania	Албания	albanija
Bulgaria	Болгария	bolgarija
Hungary	Венгрия	vengrija

Latvia	**Латвия**	latvija
Lithuania	**Литва**	litva
Poland	**Польша**	polʲʃa

Romania	**Румыния**	rumınija
Serbia	**Сербия**	serbija
Slovakia	**Словакия**	slovakija

Croatia	**Хорватия**	xorvatija
Czech Republic	**Чехия**	ʧexija
Estonia	**Эстония**	estonija

Bosnia and Herzegovina	**Босния жана**	bosnija ʤana
Macedonia (Republic of ~)	**Македония**	makedonija
Slovenia	**Словения**	slovenija
Montenegro	**Черногория**	ʧernogorija

149. Former USSR countries

| Azerbaijan | **Азербайжан** | azerbajʤan |
| Armenia | **Армения** | armenija |

Belarus	**Беларусь**	belarusʲ
Georgia	**Грузия**	gruzija
Kazakhstan	**Казакстан**	kazakstan
Kirghizia	**Кыргызстан**	kırgızstan
Moldova, Moldavia	**Молдова**	moldova

| Russia | **Россия** | rossija |
| Ukraine | **Украина** | ukraina |

Tajikistan	**Тажикистан**	taʤikistan
Turkmenistan	**Туркмения**	turkmenija
Uzbekistan	**Өзбекистан**	øzbekistan

150. Asia

Asia	**Азия**	azija
Vietnam	**Вьетнам**	vjetnam
India	**Индия**	indija
Israel	**Израиль**	izrailʲ

China	**Кытай**	kıtaj
Lebanon	**Ливан**	livan
Mongolia	**Монголия**	mongolija

| Malaysia | **Малазия** | malazija |
| Pakistan | **Пакистан** | pakistan |

Saudi Arabia	Сауд Аравиясы	saud aravijası
Thailand	Таиланд	tailand
Taiwan	Тайвань	tajvanʲ
Turkey	Түркия	tyrkija
Japan	Япония	japonija

Afghanistan	Ооганстан	ooganstan
Bangladesh	Бангладеш	bangladeʃ
Indonesia	Индонезия	indonezija
Jordan	Иордания	iordanija

Iraq	Ирак	irak
Iran	Иран	iran
Cambodia	Камбожа	kambodʒa
Kuwait	Кувейт	kuvejt

Laos	Лаос	laos
Myanmar	Мьянма	mjanma
Nepal	Непал	nepal
United Arab Emirates	Бириккен Араб Эмираттары	birikken arab emirattarı

Syria	Сирия	sirija
Palestine	Палестина	palestina
South Korea	Түштүк Корея	tyʃtyk koreja
North Korea	Түндүк Корея	tundyk koreja

151. North America

United States of America	Америка Кошмо Штаттары	amerika koʃmo ʃtattarı
Canada	Канада	kanada
Mexico	Мексика	meksika

152. Central and South America

Argentina	Аргентина	argentina
Brazil	Бразилия	brazilija
Colombia	Колумбия	kolumbija
Cuba	Куба	kuba
Chile	Чили	tʃili

Bolivia	Боливия	bolivija
Venezuela	Венесуэла	venesuela
Paraguay	Парагвай	paragvaj
Peru	Перу	peru
Suriname	Суринам	surinam
Uruguay	Уругвай	urugvaj

Ecuador	Эквадор	ekvador
The Bahamas	Багам аралдары	bagam araldarı
Haiti	Гаити	gaiti
Dominican Republic	Доминикан Республикасы	dominikan respublikası
Panama	Панама	panama
Jamaica	Ямайка	jamajka

153. Africa

Egypt	Египет	egipet
Morocco	Марокко	marokko
Tunisia	Тунис	tunis
Ghana	Гана	gana
Zanzibar	Занзибар	zanzibar
Kenya	Кения	kenija
Libya	Ливия	livija
Madagascar	Мадагаскар	madagaskar
Namibia	Намибия	namibija
Senegal	Сенегал	senegal
Tanzania	Танзания	tanzanija
South Africa	ТАР	tar

154. Australia. Oceania

Australia	Австралия	avstralija
New Zealand	Жаңы Зеландия	dʒaŋı zelandija
Tasmania	Тасмания	tasmanija
French Polynesia	Француз Полинезиясы	frantsuz polinezijası

155. Cities

Amsterdam	Амстердам	amsterdam
Ankara	Анкара	ankara
Athens	Афина	afina
Baghdad	Багдад	bagdad
Bangkok	Бангкок	bangkok
Barcelona	Барселона	barselona
Beijing	Пекин	pekin
Beirut	Бейрут	bejrut
Berlin	Берлин	berlin

| Bonn | Бонн | bonn |
| Bordeaux | Бордо | bordo |

Bratislava	Братислава	bratislava
Brussels	Брюссель	brusselʲ
Bucharest	Бухарест	buχarest
Budapest	Будапешт	budapeʃt
Cairo	Каир	kair

Chicago	Чикаго	tʃikago
Copenhagen	Копенгаген	kopengagen
Dar-es-Salaam	Дар-эс-Салам	dar-es-salam
Delhi	Дели	deli
Dubai	Дубай	dubaj

Dublin	Дублин	dublin
Düsseldorf	Дюссельдорф	dusselʲdorf
Florence	Флоренция	florentsija
Frankfurt	Франкфурт	frankfurt
Geneva	Женева	dʒeneva

Hamburg	Гамбург	gamburg
Hanoi	Ханой	χanoj
Havana	Гавана	gavana
Helsinki	Хельсинки	χelʲsinki
Hiroshima	Хиросима	χirosima

Hong Kong	Гонконг	gonkong
Istanbul	Стамбул	stambul
Jerusalem	Иерусалим	ierusalim
Kolkata (Calcutta)	Калькутта	kalʲkutta
Kuala Lumpur	Куала-Лумпур	kuala-lumpur

Kyiv	Киев	kiev
Lisbon	Лиссабон	lissabon
London	Лондон	london
Los Angeles	Лос-Анджелес	los-andʒeles
Lyons	Лион	lion
Madrid	Мадрид	madrid

Marseille	Марсель	marselʲ
Mexico City	Мехико	meχiko
Miami	Майями	majami
Montreal	Монреаль	monrealʲ
Moscow	Москва	moskva

Mumbai (Bombay)	Бомбей	bombej
Munich	Мюнхен	munχen
Nairobi	Найроби	najrobi
Naples	Неаполь	neapolʲ
New York	Нью-Йорк	nju-jork
Nice	Ницца	nitstsa

Oslo	Осло	oslo
Ottawa	Оттава	ottava
Paris	Париж	paridʒ
Prague	Прага	praga

Rio de Janeiro	Рио-де-Жанейро	rio-de-dʒanejro
Rome	Рим	rim
Saint Petersburg	Санкт-Петербург	sankt-peterburg
Seoul	Сеул	seul
Shanghai	Шанхай	ʃanχaj

Singapore	Сингапур	singapur
Stockholm	Стокгольм	stokgolʲm
Sydney	Сидней	sidnej
Taipei	Тайпей	tajpej
The Hague	Гаага	gaaga
Tokyo	Токио	tokio

Toronto	Торонто	toronto
Venice	Венеция	venetsija
Vienna	Вена	vena
Warsaw	Варшава	varʃava
Washington	Вашингтон	waʃington

www.ingramcontent.com/pod-product-compliance
Lightning Source LLC
Chambersburg PA
CBHW061953070426
42450CB00011BA/2811